One More Chance

The real life adventures of an animal rescuer and
the experiences that changed her life forever

Kari D Thompson

7/20/17

Linnie,

You and I are healers,
We give and expect nothing
in return.

Our gift is, love, Compassion,
And a Willingness to help.

"How is it that animals understand things
I do not know, but it is certain that they do
understand. Perhaps there is a language which
is not made of words and everything in the world
understands it. Perhaps there is a soul hidden
in everything and it can always speak, without
ever making a sound, to another soul." Frances
Hodgson Burnett.

With love to my dear healing
friend ~

Lisa Thompson

2

Gypsy Raven Press

Copyright © Kari D Thompson 2011

Note to the reader: This book is intended as an informational guide. The remedies, approaches, and techniques described herein are meant to supplement, and not to be a substitute for professional veterinary care or treatment. They should not be used to treat a serious ailment without prior consultation with a state-licensed veterinarian. ***Never approach an injured animal without proper training, protective gear, vaccinations and back-up assistance.***

Cover Design: Cover Creator, Photo collage: Deborah L Townsend
Text design and layout: Kari D Thompson
Editing: Michelle Parnell Rohrer
Photographic credits: Kari D Thompson, Deborah L Townsend
Photo of Maggie: Mary Blanton
Three Doggies: Michelle Parnell Rohrer

This book was typeset in Times New Roman, Bazooka and Arial

Distributed by amazon.com and other retailers.
Distributed to the book trade in the United States of America

ISBN 1-451-51534-0
Printed in the United States of America
10 9 8 7 6 5 4 3 2 1

First Edition

To those I love

My precious mother Alexis; who always encourages whatever I choose to do. Thank you for giving me the encouragement and love to become who I am and for continually reminding me "you need to write". Well Mom, I did!

My beautiful and talented sister Debbie, whose unconditional love, keen photographic sense and graphic design has given artistic beauty not only to this book, but also to my life. You are my inspiration and my best friend, my little "tittu."

And lastly, my patient and loving husband Michael, for "putting up" with every imaginable injured creature and lovingly, always helping me, help them.

If all the Beasts were gone,
Men would die
from a great loneliness of
spirit.
For whatever happens to
the Beasts,
also happens to the Man.

All things are connected.

Whatever befalls the Earth,
befalls the Sons of the
Earth.

Chief Seattle of the Squamish Tribe,
Letter to President Franklin Pierce

Contents

Introduction
By Annie Bowes, D.V.M.

Preface

Chapter One: You've got to start somewhere
"Mom, I found a baby Bird"	13
Why I rescue and rehab animals	18

Chapter Two: Alternative Healing
Do herbal remedies work on pets and rescued animals?	25
Couscous	27
Little Boy	31
Doggies with Issues	36
Cheyenne	41

Chapter Three: Wonders of Nature in your yard
Bats in the barn roof	44
Sara	49
Oh Deer!!	52
Rascally Raccoon	58

Chapter Four: Opossums, opossums everywhere
The Doctors office	64
The Fatal Bite	68
An Opossum named Pocket	72

Chapter Five: Take these broken wings
The Swallows of the University	77

Wa'ipi Kwinaa (Woman Bird)   **80**
Panic on the Pier   **87**
Gregory   **90**
Willow   **95**

Chapter Six: Sad Tails, Happy Endings

Angie   **99**
Huckleberry Jazzmean, the kitten from Hades   **101**
Chi's in need   **107**
For the love of Lucy   **111**

Chapter Seven: Imprinting and Education Animals

On Education birds   **114**
The Rat Pack Crows   **115**
Tyto   **119**
We'jompe   **124**

Appendix

Rescue Basics   **131**
So, you want to volunteer?   **133**
Wild Things   **135**
Rat Poison: Often fatal results to animals   **137**
Lightning, Firecrackers & other noise phobias   **141**
Rescue Recipes   **144**

Resources   146

Acknowledgments   147

Index   150

Coming Soon   154

Introduction
By Annie Bowes, D.V.M.

Rescue and rehabilitation of wild animals is not for the faint of heart. One must bear the burden of knowing that life and possible death, rests not only in your hands, but also in your decisions for a very fragile creature, frightened beyond belief.

You may suppose the task is thankless, especially knowing that most rehabilitated animals are returned to the wild where they never look back on civilization, and retain no shred of domesticity or tameness. But as you read Kari Thompson's stories, these real life adventures of an animal rescuer, you will see that every attempt does have its rewards. Every creature will thank its rescuer in its own way.

As you travel through the stories in this book it is hoped that you will find the same sweet treasure that all animal rescuers share; the satisfaction of trying; of giving that animal "one more chance". As you read her stories and take a peek into her life, I hope you are able to see the incredible strength and gentleness that makes her who she is, which is much more than just an animal rescuer. Kari Thompson is the champion for the meek and mild creatures that have been placed in her path. Kari Thompson's stories of rescue and healing will help you understand why every life should get just "one more chance". You never know how it will bless you.

Dr. Annie Bowes hails from a long line of medicine and animal care, being Native American and raised within the healers of her tribe, then as a graduate of Washington State University College of Veterinary Medicine. As a licensed veterinarian, Dr. Bowes dedicates her life to emergency medicine in the Pacific Northwest and promotes the country way of life by providing mobile veterinary care to livestock. She raises horses, cattle, poultry and commercial hay together with her husband and best friend, Police Officer Pete Bowes. They live on the prairie of Post Falls, Idaho, where they hunt, fish, camp and enjoy the great outdoors.

Preface

As I began documenting these stories some 15 years ago, it was mainly for my own research and a way to look back on the many creatures I had the privilege of helping.

At the time I had no intention of writing a book about being a rescuer. In fact, I was convinced that people just weren't interested in what "we" do; instead I felt that the general public thought us a rather strange breed. Strange indeed! Yes, we climb mountains, scale walls, or plunge into icy waters. We dodge traffic on main thoroughfares, carry wounded animals in our arms for countless hours or sacrifice part of our clothing to create a makeshift sling or bandage to help stabilize the wounded animal. Our clothing is often soaked in blood or feces and more often than not, we get covered in ticks and mites while being clawed, bit, pecked and regurgitated upon. Why do we do this? *(I have often asked this of myself.)* Because it is in our blood and in our psyche to rescue, even when we may unknowingly put ourselves in danger.

The life of an animal rescuer is far from boring, average or routine. The make-up of a rescuer is varied and not limited to age, size race, or physical ability. One common factor though, is the unconditional love of animals and the desire to give them "one more chance". Often people will say we are obsessed with rescuing. Perhaps that is true. It is quite addicting. And yes, there are side effects: joy, sorrow and wonder, mixed with grief, pain, serenity and fulfillment, in helping Mother Nature's creatures.

Each time we help one of these animals, we connect in spirit. We help them, they teach us and we take what they give us and become better people.

In today's busy, go there, get there, no-time for that

society, the unfortunate common thread is, *"there is nothing you can do, let them die."* But that is not the case in over 60-70% of rescues! Within the human species most of *us* will do anything for "one more chance." Risk surgery, submit to radiation and endure chemo, if it means extending our lives just a bit longer. In rescue, we make the choices and take the risks for these animals to give them their second chance at life. The successes outweigh the failures. And believe it or not, they do appreciate what we do for them, as you will see.

Within these pages you will walk along side and live the life of a wildlife rescuer. Be prepared for a bumpy, scary, bittersweet yet rewarding ride that will take you places in your heart and mind you never thought possible.

It is with hope that these true stories will inspire you to, if nothing more, appreciates the men, women, children and youth who volunteer countless hours and give up normalcy in their lives, all for animals, to give them, one more chance.

Chapter One

You've got to start somewhere!

"I could not have slept tonight if I had left the helpless little creature to perish on the ground".
The reply President Abraham Lincoln gave his friends as he stopped to return a fledgling to its nest.

"Mom, I found a baby bird"

From a very early age, as far back as I can remember, I have been "finding" injured animals. Or as I have discovered, they have been "finding me."

My first experience was the catalyst that propelled me into the realm of an animal rescuer and advocate. Though at the time, I was too young to know how this tiny fragile bird would forever change my life.

It was a warm spring day in Concord California. The vivid blue sky was dotted with fluffy white clouds. I, a nine year old, rather prissy girlie girl, in nicely pressed crisp clean trousers, my blouse new and neat, and my long brown hair pulled back into a nice ponytail, lay outside on my back taking in the sweet smells of a newly mowed lawn. My dad told me that clouds told stories and if you looked closely, you would see the stories come to life. Well, I was ready for some stories. The clouds slowly moved into shapes and faces. I pretended that I was a princess being rescued from the dragon that was swooping down and as he faded away, I became a mermaid, swimming alongside a rather fat laughing dolphin.

Birds fluttered to and fro from the trees and a soft breeze was blowing. In the distance I heard what sounded like a "beep, beep, beep," a minute sound somewhere not too far from where I was laying. I averted my gaze from the Indian on horseback that floated through the sky and focused my attention to the whereabouts of the "beep, beep, beep." Where is it coming from I wondered?

My German Shepherd Prince suddenly began barking at a nearby juniper bush. "Beep, beep, beep" went the sound again; Prince was barking like crazy, all the while wagging his tail. "Shush, Prince, you'll scare it," I scolded. Down on my knees looking under the bush, I didn't see anything at first, just

13

a lot of moist dirt and bugs moving around. "I hate bugs," I said aloud. Prince nosed next to me and sniffed loudly. "OK, OK, I'm looking," I said. Slowly I crawled further under the bush, pushing aside the icky bugs with my bare hands. "Eww." Then I saw a tiny little "thing" move. "Oh I see it," I squealed, "I see it Prince, it's a baby bird!"

I reached in and picked up the tiny little thing. I was so frightened that I might hurt it. Gently, I cradled this tiny bit of life in my hands as I crawled out from under the bush. My clothes were covered in dirt with squished bugs on my knees. I didn't seem to notice as I held this precious little baby in my hands. Suddenly, it began flapping its wings. The tiny beak was open wide and the bird cried "BEEP, BEEP, BEEP". I was so scared that I almost dropped it. Prince nosed my hand to see the tiny creature, keeping me from opening my hands too wide. "Get away, Prince, it's really cold. I need to go tell Mom and see what to do".

Running into the kitchen I cried, "Mom, I found a baby bird." My mother was chopping vegetables and turned to look at me. "Kari, what in the world, you're filthy", she said somewhat sternly. "I know mom, but"... I stammered. "No buts, let's get you out of those dirty clothes". "Mom, I found a baby bird, see?" I opened my dirty hands and the little bird began flapping its wings and beeping loudly. Tears welled up in my eyes as I looked at her. "What can we do, mom? It's cold and hungry". I pleaded. "OK honey, I don't really know what to do" she said. "Mom...?" "OK, let me get a kitchen towel and put it here on the counter by the stove, where it's warm. You go and look for a shoe box and I will call Nana and ask her?"

Nana was from Alabama and had been raised on a farm. Most of her youth had been spent working with animals. She was a wealth of information, even though she only went through the fourth grade. She could barely write and took her time reading, but she was great with old folk remedies for

14

everything under the sun. If anyone would know, it would be Nana. "Yippee! Nana will know what to do, won't she mom?" Mom looked at me, smiling, she said, "I hope so, now go get a shoe box and while you're at it, get into some clean clothes, we have company coming this evening". "It's going to live isn't it mom?" I begged. "It's going to live right?" My mother was used to me bringing stray puppies and kittens home, but a baby bird, this was new for her as well. She did her best to reassure me and I scampered off in search of a shoe box.

She called my Nana and within a few minutes Nana had given her the basics of baby bird care. As I rushed into the kitchen, mom hung up the phone and gave me instructions as to what to do for the bird. We mixed up tiny bits of bread with luke warm milk and gently fed the baby with a pair of tweezers. It flapped its wings and took the food in. I was so excited, but scared too. Mom said it was enough food, and I protested. "The baby's beak is still open! It's still hungry." "Kari, we don't want to over feed it, and that's enough for now. Let's get it covered and in a nice warm place. Also, leave it alone and don't bother it. The baby bird needs rest." Mom told me that Nana has said we needed to look for the nest tomorrow and put the baby back. "What?" I protested. "We can't, it will starve, or Prince will find it, or it will be too cold, or fall out of the nest again or…" "Shush honey; it's the right thing to do". She looked at me and smiled.

Mom was right, as always, it was the best thing to do. The very next morning we went outside, and my little sister Debbie found the nest with another baby bird inside. My mom and sister looked as I gently placed the baby back into the nest. Momma bird was fretting and flying from branch to branch, urging me to go away.

I wanted to stay and watch the baby, but my mom urged me to leave the nest alone and let the momma bird take care of its young. "Will it live mom?" I asked with big tears rolling down my freckled cheeks. "I think it stands a good chance, now let's get ready for our picnic at Nana's house".

Many weeks went by and the little birds grew and took on the look of their parents. One day I went out to check the nest and they were gone. I came inside crying and told my mom that they had disappeared. She said that birds fly from their nests and go to warmer places when fall comes. "Will I ever see it again?" I asked. "Maybe honey." That answer didn't really satisfy me, but I knew she was right and that the bird deserved to fly and not be in a cage or worse.

One fall afternoon, I lay watching the clouds move at a fast pace. The leaves had turned golden and the wind took on a crisp snap. In the clouds, an old man grinned and in an instant his face grew long and into that of a wolf. Three round mounds of clouds turned into penguins moving like bowling pins. The wind seems to move them swiftly, creating new faces every few seconds. A very distinctive cloud transformed into a longhaired gypsy. She danced round and round and suddenly out of her hands flew a bird; the clouds had formed a perfect little bird, my rescue bird. The little cloud bird turned to me and smiled and in an instant, the wind carried her off to warmer places and a new life. Tears wet my cheeks, not from sadness, but, the child I was knew suddenly that clouds do tell stories and that little girls can do small things that make a difference.

This baby mocking bird was found at the base of a tree where its nest had been torn from the limb it rested on, presumably by a cat. Only two of the four survived the attack

Why rescue and rehab Animals?

Wild animals are brought into rehabilitation/wildlife care centers suffering from numerous afflictions. Often they can result from natural disasters, accidents, outbreaks of disease, but the largest percentage are injured, sick and orphaned due (either directly or indirectly) to the human animal.

After my childhood experience with the little bird, I tended to be involved with animals of every kind. My Nana had a houseful of dogs and I would work with her helping with the birth of puppies and caring for them when she became ill. Nana taught me patience with animals. Being a Type A child, I was always busy and helping her with the dogs calmed me down and gave me something new and exciting to learn.

I learned from my personal experience of the little bird, that during breeding season, many dependant young animals can be secondary victims of incidents that killed their parents or they can be "rescued" by well meaning people who do not understand the natural behaviors of wildlife. Then there are poachers that steal babies from nests, dens and anywhere they can find a "marketable" animal that is rare or exotic and will sell them on the underground market. Thankfully, many find their way into a rescue facility, though often abused, neglected and in desperate need of long-term foster care, are given one more chance at life. Then there are animals that just need someone to give a little extra care.

Our High School had an iguana named Iggy Sue. Much to the dismay of my mother, I brought Iggy Sue home for the summer. She was a really cool iguana. I would take her for walks on a leash, let her run in the backyard and catch bugs. She was like a really freaky-looking dog and my time with her helped me over my phobia of reptiles, sort of.

One summer my sister and I received two female mice as pets. The pet-store owner swore that he had kept the males and females separate. NOT! Shortly after we got our new friends home, they had babies, and then their babies had babies and within three months we had over 50 mice. It was insane. We would try and separate them and WHAM, another litter of pinkies!(Baby mice are born with no fur and are a light pink color, hence the name pinkies). Fortunately, we got a bunch of cages from a friend and were finally able to separate them. We had moved them into the garage because the smell was overwhelming, to say the least!

One Saturday morning I went out to check their water and food. My mouse Squeaky and Deb's mouse Gretchen were frozen, not from the cold, but hypnotized by the rhythmic moving of a garden snake. I of course, screamed and ran inside the house. Our neighbor across the street heard the commotion and came over to see what was wrong. She, a grade school teacher immediately grabbed the snake. It bit her on her middle finger, which began to swell. She smiled and said "I will take this to school on Monday for the kids to see." She didn't even flinch at the bite.

After the snake incident, Mom and Dad said we had to find homes for the mice. Squeaky and Gretchen had died from their trauma, and Deb and I were sad about that, so it wasn't a hard decision to find homes for 48 mice, we didn't want to go through that again. In fact, I took them to school and by the end of the day each had found a new home. It was a good lesson for us to learn about the care of mice and how quickly they breed. We were confident that no females were pregnant, because we had kept them separated, which was what parents wanted to hear as they took the mice home.

When I completed high school we moved to Hawaii and became interested in horses. My sister was taking riding lessons along with my dad so naturally we ended up with a horse, a thoroughbred named Hula Bye. The care of the horse became a priority and soon Deb and I were mucking out stalls and being ranch hands. The ranch had their share of stray dogs and cats that had wandered in and of course, I rescued a couple of them.

When I moved back to the mainland, my family bought some additional horses and then rescued a couple of goats, and so on. Within six months we had a farm with lots of animals to care for. I became comfortable with foaling and was excellent at bottle-feeding baby goats.

My parents were always supportive of my little critters and their encouragement kept me focused. When I met and married my husband Michael, he wasn't too sure in the beginning about the rescuing, but when he saw how it touched me and that we were making a difference, he too became caught up in my passion.

One of our mares had a difficult pregnancy and delivered a still-borne foal. I was assisting and the smell of the foal was all over me. When Michael removed the dead foal, the mare began nudging me to move around the pen. She didn't seem to notice that I was human; she just smelled her baby and urged me to move. We had a couple of ranch hands that knew of an orphaned filly. Mom called the rancher and asked if he had found a mare to suckle his orphaned foal. He had not. They both agreed that he would bring the newborn filly over in the morning. The problem with that was, the mare thinking I was her baby kept me moving all night. By the time the rancher arrived with the orphaned foal, I was bruised, exhausted and famished. It was amazing to see how, after I rubbed the scent from me on the orphan, that our mare began nosing her and doing what she had been doing to me. The orphan began to suckle and all was well.

The orphaned filly and new momma.

I continued to rescue birds and other animals and when I was not rescuing, I volunteered my time at the Wild Life Network. There I learned how to handle raptors, opossum, ring tailed cats, raccoons, woodpeckers and everything in between. That volunteer experience was better than any training I could have paid for and the hands on experience built up my skills and gave me confidence with a variety of wild animals.

Not every rescue has a happy ending. We have lost many animals from severe head injuries, cancer, poisoning, trauma, animal attacks, old age and other ailments. You become attached to them and even though you try everything you know of to try and save them, if they die you feel like a part of you dies also. Rescuing is very emotional and can be bittersweet. But I rescue because it is part of who I am. I give 100% to the animals in my care, because I have a strong desire to use my gifts as a healer. The successes outweigh the failures and so actually, there are no failures, just unsuccessful attempts, at saving a life.

I have been asked numerous times, how I deal with loss and not carry the depression around inside. To be honest, I cry a lot. You never get over the loss of a rescue animal, but you cope knowing that you did everything possible to *try* and save a life. None of us are miracle workers, our hearts are in the right place seeking to help and each time we succeed, it helps for the times we do not. I just say a silent prayer and ask God to bless them and then with peace in my heart, I let it go.

My desire to rescue seems to be out there in the universal cosmos. Animals find me. I open my back door and there is a tiny kitten sitting there helpless. A mangy flea bitten puppy will find its way onto the property. While driving into town on the side of the road will be an injured crow, or raccoon. Such is the life of this rescuer. It gives me a sense of purpose. I make a difference and the pay back is joy and fulfillment. I have been blessed with the unique talent of being an intuitive healer and have a great deal of compassion for our four legged and winged friends.

I suppose that I will be doing this for the rest of my life. I honestly can't imagine my life without some sort of rescue or rehab going on. All of my dogs, cats, birds and even chickens are rescues. Come to think of it, some of my friends are rescues, too!

God gave me this ability to help and the talents to care for those in need. I take that *very* seriously.

My mom says that from birth I have loved animals; always reaching out to touch.

By age two I was "grooming" neighborhood dogs, unafraid.

Chapter Two

Alternative Healing

"The question is not "Can they reason?" nor "Can they think?"
but rather, "Can they suffer?"

Jeremy Bentham

Do herbal remedies work on pets and rescued animals?

The answer to this is a resounding YES! In the wild animals will use their natural instincts to find healing herbs to ease their ailments. Nature has always held the answers and the medicine cabinet of trees, plants, berries and other natural flora and fauna is abundant, even in our own backyard.

Have you ever had a dog or cat that goes out and eats grass and then within a few minutes promptly will throw it up? This is an instinctual way of cleaning their system. Cats do it to assist in getting rid of hairballs; dogs do it to clean their stomachs. It's instinctive.

Pollution, stress, environmental changes, poor nutrition and unhealthy lifestyles can lead to illness and dis-ease in animals of all types, similar to those experienced by humans. Herbal remedies like homeopathy, tinctures, Bach Flower remedies and others are not unpleasant and offer no dangerous side effects when administered correctly, while achieving successful results. Often an animal will respond in a more favorable manner to the natural remedy than a prescribed drug and will take it more readily.

Many veterinarians are now using homeopathy and naturopathy to their regime of treatments with great success and you can find in larger cities veterinarians that specialize in alternative healing practices. There are acupuncturists, animal massage therapists, Reiki practitioners, pet psychologists and many other healers offering alternative methods to animals that are suffering.

In rescue and rehab we have limited access to qualified vets who understand the complexities of injured wildlife or who will risk treating an injured raptor for instance, because of

State and Federal regulations. Their expertise usually is on domestics and livestock, leaving the rescuer to his or her own devices. All qualified rescuers have undergone some type of training, either with the International Wildlife Rehabilitation Council (IWRC) or through Fish and Game and have a permit to rescue and rehab. We believe that using natural remedies to treat wild animals seems only, well, natural. In the wild they seek it out, so in rescue we try and provide the same. Many of us have our kitchens or rescue rooms stocked with healing herbs, aromatherapy, and homeopathy and even flower remedies.

While we utilize nature's medicine chest, we also rely on our veterinary friends to give their knowledge and life saving talents to our injured friends. We form a cooperative balance of allopathic (regular medical doctors) and naturopathic (unconventional, herbal or "faith") healing, which greatly enhances the survival rate of our patients.

The use of homeopathic, herbs, aromatherapy and other modems of healing should not be used by those with little to no knowledge of their healing properties. Many plants can heal or hurt, depending on their dosage. Please contact a qualified veterinarian or Holistic Practitioner if in doubt before administering treatment.

Couscous

My telephone was constantly ringing. "Kari? This is Terri. I see you are home", she said a bit irritated. "Well yes" I said, "I am and have been here all day getting ready for the party, what's up?" I asked. "Please open your front door and look in your driveway" she said with a chill in her voice. "Ah...OK". I opened the door and there sat Terri in her van, in my driveway, on her cell phone. "OK Terri, what's your point?" I queried. "My point is, I have been knocking on your door for 10 minutes and..." I broke into laughter and waved her inside and hung up the phone.

Terri was not the only person to phone me from my driveway. I had become so accustomed to the sound of my rescued woodpecker's drumming that I hardly ever opened the door, because I thought it was Cousie! My rescue bird Couscous (Cousie for short), an Acorn Woodpecker had her living environment in the sunroom and being a woodpecker, she would make a drumming sound all day. It was more of a bang, bang, and a tap-tap bang-bang along with her vocal repertoire of "whack-a-whack-a" and a fast paced "cous-cous-cous" hence her name. Terri was greeted by a cacophony of sounds as she entered the room. We both stood laughing at this tiny red headed bird with a big heart and an even bigger beak.

Nine years prior, a little boy on his way home from school had rescued Cousie. At the base of a palm tree he found this tiny little bird unable to fly and falling over. The young boy picked her up and took her to the wildlife rescue. I happened to be volunteering that day and along with many others, we eagerly took in the bird and I began accessing her condition. It was an exceptionally busy spring day with baby birds coming in about every 10 minutes. One of the other ladies talked with the young boy and soon he was gone.

I had been training on woodpeckers and it was agreed that I would take this little one home to rehab, if possible. After careful examination, it appeared that Cousie suffered from a neurological condition that quite possibly had short-circuited her ability to be in an upright position. I had been actively using homeopathic remedies to treat barn owls and others with head trauma with about a 65-70% success rate, so I began Cousie on a regime of Arnica Montana, Hypericum and Bach Flower Remedy. Within two days she was sitting upright and was beginning to try and eat on her own (which I was grateful for. Tube feeding a woodpecker is not easy and their long hard beaks really hurt). I hoped that within a few weeks she would be able to be released.

I phoned the center and asked for the location of where the boy had found her. The voice on the other end was unsure and could find no intake report, just a notation in the logbook stating 'very *busy today, took in injured woodpecker, Kari to rehab.*' There was no name, no location, nothing to identify where the bird came from. I was discouraged with that bit of news, but very pleased with the progress of Cousie, so I decided that, if she recovered, we would find a solution for her at that time. Woodpeckers are not only hard to rehab, but they live in colonies and have to be re-released back where they came from, or they will be killed by a rival colony.

Several months went by and each day Cousie became stronger. She was gobbling up mealworms and the formula we fed to injured birds. She loved peanuts and would crack them open with one blow of her strong beak and torment the nut for hours. She had gained weight and was upright. I had discontinued the Hypericum and Arnica after 30 days seeing excellent improvement. The dilemma facing me now was, where would she be released?

The Wildlife Network had many ladies that rescued woodpeckers, so I got a phone chain going on as to what to do with this issue. We brainstormed and unfortunately, came to the conclusion that Cousie could not be released. The ideal situation and what all rehabbers aspire to; is to be able to release the rescued animals back to nature, where they came from and where they need to be. Cousie's original rescue spot had not been identified, so that left us with two choices: euthanasia or take her on as a permanent 'education bird.' We all agreed and opted for the latter and Cousie became an ambassador to children and adults alike.

For nine years Cousie delighted kids at school. She enjoyed her outings and didn't mind the kids peering at her. She would contently bang and make her whack-a-whack-a sounds and loved her treats of mealworms and grasshoppers. She was not a pet, nor was she treated as one. She was, however a wonderful friend and a great ambassador to the public. The sad part of that being, she grew up thinking of me as her mother and never knew her own kind. As her caregiver I tried to give her the best life possible, in an environment that was comfortable and as close to her natural habitat as possible. Her life was filled with good food, lots of room to fly and play and of course, lots of love.

One morning I got up and went into the kitchen to make a cup of tea. It was oddly still and quiet. Immediately I rushed over to Cousie's cage. There she lay, forever quiet. The stillness of the house was maddening and I wept like a baby. Even now, how I long to hear the sounds she used to make.

In the spring I go outside and watch the parents of local hatchling woodpeckers feed their young. I listen to the sounds they make as they chatter back and forth. Cousie taught me a lot about this species. They are fiercely loyal, hard workers and have a sense of humor, almost where you might call them clowns. As a rescuer, the greatest joy is to release an animal back into nature, but when you have ambassador animals that you care for, they become part of your family and their loss is felt deeply.

Cousie was and is a testament to the successful use of homeopathic medicines and I have since treated many birds and mammals with homeopathy, Bach Flower remedies and herbology addressing neurological and other issues with a high degree of success.

Couscous in her living environment

Woodpeckers are colony dwellers. They can often be heard on the telephone poles "drumming," making a loud sound that calls others near. The "drumming" can be a warning of trouble, or to attract mates. Their beaks are very hard and can make nesting holes in a tree in just a few hours.

Little Boy

Early on a misty April morning my friend Connie from the network stood at my front door. In her hands was a tiny injured opossum. "I think something bit him, Kari, you're really good with them and I have too many birds right now to give him the attention he needs." Connie said in almost a whisper. I looked at the tiny little thing and agreed to take him in for rehab.

Immediately I took his temperature, cleaned the wound, checked him over for any other wounds. I noticed that he was missing two digits on his right paw. I then wrapped him in a towel. My gas stove was nice and warm on the top, so I placed him gently down with some fleece underneath to keep him comfortable. Connie stayed for a cup of tea, and then went back to her menagerie of over 100 birds. The little opossum was very lethargic and I knew that this wouldn't be an easy fix, if he could be fixed at all.

His puncture wound was in the shoulder area and it seemed that he was not able to use his paws. I started him on Hypericum and Arnica Montana, with rescue remedy as well. Little Boy had to be fed with a syringe at first. Within two days he was sitting up, eating yogurt and scrambled eggs. He was alert, but unable to completely move his hindquarters. I had to poop and pee him, clean him up and make sure he was comfortable. After two days I called Dr. Beth at the vet clinic and told her what was going on with Little Boy. We both agreed he needed to be seen and evaluated. Beth checked him over and called in another vet. They felt that he might regain use of his legs with proper exercise and plenty of rest. The bite may or may not have injured his spinal column. He was not paralyzed, just partially functioning.

On the way home he crawled out of his blanket and drug himself into my lap. I gently rubbed his tiny head as I drove home. My heart hurt looking at this little baby, so beautiful and loving and yet so vulnerable and needy. I knew that I needed outside help, but from whom?

Little Boy was hungry when we got home, so I fixed his formula, gave him some grapes and some mealworms, along with the homeopathic regime. Beth had given me some antibiotics as well to stave off any infection that might occur from the bite. I always made sure that while giving antibiotics that yogurt was introduced into the diet, to help eliminate the overabundance of yeast in the body. Opossums love yogurt! When he was cleaned up and resting, I got on the computer and began researching injuries such as his. What was surprising to me, and it came up almost instantly, was a healing practice called reiki. Reiki is a healing method using energy. Although it does not require touch, the energy creates a sense of peace and tranquility and healing seems to come naturally. I read of the success of other rehabbers and the use of the energy of Reiki as a treatment. Immediately I got off the computer, opened my phone book and called Allison. We had met at a rescue meeting just a couple of weeks past. She was a Level Three Master Reiki healer. We talked about little boy and Allison agreed to come the following day and give him a treatment.

Allison arrived around noon. I brought out Little Boy and she sat and looked at him. Tears filled her eyes. "I think I can help, but I sense there is something else going on with him" she said. "What do you mean something else?" I asked. "Well, let me work with him and I will let you know". I looked at her and nodded. She then took a long time concentrating and moving her hands over his tiny body. I was amazed to see him move as her hands passed over his hind legs. She didn't touch him, just used energy to re-balance him. He was very alert and moving all over, not walking, but trying to. I was astounded to see this type of progress in just a half hour!

"Kari, Reiki energy stimulates the energy into the

32

neural-pathways of the body and brings healing to any area that is needed. Your little guy has some severe trauma to his spinal cord, but I believe with continued treatments and the homeopathy you are doing, he can make a partial if not full recovery." Allison smiled. *'Partial,* if not full recovery.' The words resounded in my head but then I thought, at least it was something. He wasn't in pain and seemed to be getting stronger. We set up a treatment schedule for the next couple of weeks to try and help Little Boy.

Over the next months, Little Boy got stronger. My husband Michael had become so fond of him that he took over his nightly feedings. He grew but was still unable to walk. He played with toys with his front paws, enjoyed his food and showed great attachment to Michael. We were very pleased to see the progress and Little Boy seemed content.

One morning I went in to check him and there was blood all over his face. I began checking him over and found that he had been chewing his right front paw. I immediately called Allison and she came right over. She felt that he was regaining feeling or some stimulation in his extremities and it might be painful. I was just devastated that he was self mutilating. Allison worked on him for over an hour and he seemed ok. I bandaged his paw and called Dr. Beth. I was afraid that we would have to put him down. My heart sank at the prospect of doing that, but I couldn't let him suffer. Dr. Beth told me to keep his paw wrapped and to come in and get a mild pain killer. I did and started him on that, but I also began adding Bach Rescue remedy to his yogurt as well. She and I worked on Little Boy for weeks. He rallied around and got more strength. He was growing and moving around as best as he could but was still partially paralyzed in the hind end.

It had now been seven months since Little Boy had been brought to me for rehab. He was big and sassy; eating everything he could and was playful. I would go in and sit with him for hours, just rubbing his belly, exercising his legs and loving him. I put Little Boy to bed just before my husband came home from work.

Michael walked in with a pained looked on his face and told me the news. "Our company has been sold and I have been transferred to Montana." I stood dumbfounded looking at him. "What, Montana are you kidding, what about our rescue animals, what about our house?" I cried. He stood looking at me and said we had to move within a month as his new position started at that time.

Michael moved most of our belongings to a home in Montana. I stayed behind listing our house for sale and placing the birds, raccoons and opossum I had in rehab. I cried almost every day, because I felt like I was abandoning my babies. I had crows that had come back from near death that needed special care. I had an imprinted opossum named Pocket that would sit on my lap and watch TV and then there was Little Boy. I couldn't get Fish and Game to give me permission to take the animals with me because I was going across state lines and to an area where there were no opossum and crows could be shot. I sat down and prayed. "God, please send someone to take care of the babies" I sobbed. "I just can't walk away."

I literally ran into a woman at the network office the following day. I turned around and we collided. Her name was Marilyn and she was new to the area. I had been crying and she asked me what the matter was. After I blubbered my predicament to her, she smiled and said, "I specialize in injured opossum and love crows." Marilyn was the answer to my prayers. She agreed to take Little Boy and the special needs crows and she was thrilled about Pocket!

I felt at peace leaving my babies with Marilyn and she has continued working with Allison. Little Boy lived out his life with love and was free of pain, though he never fully regained the use of his hind legs. Pocket found a fantastic new mom in Marilyn and the crows are still happy in her sanctuary.

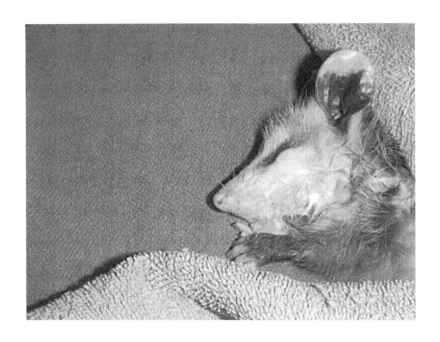

Little Boy, resting on the warmth of the stove.

Doggies with Issues

After moving to Montana and finding it not a good fit, my husband and I decided to relocate to North Idaho. Michael found a great job doing what he loves, working with aircraft. I looked at getting back into wildlife rescue. There are some very nice high-end rehab centers but none of them were near where we lived and it is VERY difficult to get a permit to rehab in Idaho and Montana for that matter. So, I did the next best thing, I applied for a kennel cleaning position at the local shelter in our small town. With my years of rehab experience, I got the job and it paid real money, though I didn't know how hard the job would be both physically and emotionally.

Shelter work is very rewarding. There are always dogs and cats in need of someone to care for them while they are waiting for placement. My paid job was to clean the kennels, my volunteer job was to vaccinate all incoming animals, transport them for spay and neutering, rescue abandoned and abused animals, give meds as needed, handle numerous phone calls looking for animals and dealing with people who had to place their animal. I also did almost all of the coordination for adoptions, wrote a weekly column called Ask Woofie and in my spare time, was their human buddy!

A frantic call came into the shelter about a dire situation asking that we rescue a momma dog and seven puppies that were languishing at a makeshift puppy mill. I consulted our Board of Directors and asked for permission to take in these dogs. They agreed. After communicating with the owner of the dogs and explaining the need for us to intervene, she reluctantly agreed and let us pick-up the poor momma and pups. The momma, who had been bred young, was terrified of people and was skin and bones and we knew it would take a lot of TLC for this dog, but all of us were prepared to give her just that.

36

We had seven dog kennels and rotated dogs in and out when adopted. As with any shelter, the demand was greater than the space in which to place them, so we always had a waiting list. We did some creative juggling and used our kennel at the back of the dog room for momma and pups. We named her Oodles, because she had oodles of puppies when she came into the shelter. She was not housebroken and would run and hide whenever anyone approached to feed her or check her pups. She was terrified of men and would tinkle all over herself and shake for hours. I found a new Reiki friend named Cynthia and asked her to come and assist with Oodles. Cynthia came with her husband Dennis, both Master Reiki healers to assess the situation.

The gentle vibrational "frequency" of energy healing, is a pain free, non-invasive and stress free treatment, making it the perfect healing tool for animals in a stress related situation. At out shelter there had been several skeptics as to the validity of Reiki, but after experiencing a session with Cynthia, the humans had come away with a new understanding of the power of this healing treatment. One volunteer experienced less pain after Cynthia worked on her back and another was relieved of a severe headache after just 30 minutes with Cynthia and the energy of Reiki. Cynthia and Dennis double whammied Oodles with loving energy. Within days she was better and would let us take her out to use the bathroom. She began responding to men, though shy at first. It was a miracle of transformation of this sweet little dog.

We weaned the pups and took Oodles in to be spayed. While waiting to pick her up, a lovely young woman named Jan came in and said that Cynthia had sent her here to see Oodles. The vet brought the still loopy dog out and she jumped into Jan's arms. I was stunned. Jan asked if she could foster Oodles and I agreed. We did paperwork in my car and Oodles was off to a new home. Within a week we received a call from an ecstatic Jan asking to adopt Oodles. She had not gone to the bathroom once inside, she was happy and played with Jan's other dogs and was content. It was a very happy ending for Oodles and for Jan, thanks to Reiki.

Not soon after Oodles left to her forever home, we had a male German shepherd dog brought in, which was suffering from signs of neglect and abuse. He would cower in the back of his kennel and soil himself. In the beginning I and a few volunteers were the only people who could get close to him the poor dog would lay his head on my lap and shake. I got on the phone to Cynthia and Dennis and asked them to come over and help this poor lad. Cynthia was so gently with him and took a long time in approaching his kennel where she and Dennis brought healing energy.

He took a little more time and was so terrified and afraid of the leash, that working with him was a real test of patience for the volunteers and I. He was given lots of attention, grooming, treats and was talked to in a very calm and gentle manner. He began trusting our group, but was still afraid of outsiders. Cynthia's work with him, again being a miracle, gave him the confidence to allow outsiders to come in, rub him, take him out on a leash and walk him. The day after his last Reiki treatment a couple came in who could not speak or hear, but they were drawn to him and him to them. Our special needy doggie went home with them to a loving and quiet environment. The Reiki treatments broke down the fear barrier and he was able to trust humans again.

He did well and lived with them for four months. An unfortunate family crisis in Europe called them home and they had to return him back to the shelter. They were devastated to have to leave him, but there was no other option. We did learn that he was housetrained but would still cower when it was feeding time, or when a leash was brought out. Dennis and Cynthia came back and worked with him more.

Cynthia cried after working with our needy doggie, because she could sense the sadness in him. All of us could see the fear in his eyes, but there was nothing we could do, except love him. Cynthia however, using the Reiki energy, was able to turn him around and what seemed to be yet another miracle, he began wagging his tail. Slowly he came up to the front of his kennel and would sniff hands and eventually would go out on a leash with someone other than myself. We felt that he was ready to be adopted again.

I had fallen in love with him and my husband loved him too, so, we adopted him. At first he was shy and would run from Michael but it's been three years now and he is the happiest dog ever. He gets along with all of the other rescue dogs and cats we have and is a great watch dog. The healing energy of Reiki made such a difference in him and whatever or whoever scared him doesn't exist any longer.

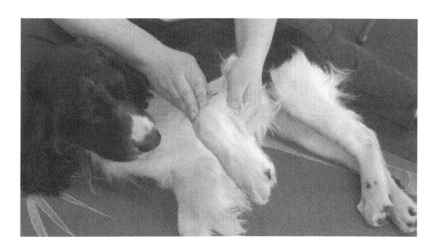

The healing power of Reiki treats an old injury.

The healing practice of Reiki has its roots in Buddhism but was rediscovered by a Christian healer by the name of Mikao Usui, the founder of the Usui System of Natural Healing in the early 20th century.

Reiki involves placing hands on or near the afflicted person or animal, starting at the head and gradually moving down the body. The Reiki practitioner feels the flow of energy and transfers that to the patient. This healing energy imparts a feeling of peace, safety, warmth and unconditional love. Reiki energy treats the inner self, the mind, body and spirit.

Cheyenne

On a whim, my mom, sister and I jumped in the car for a drive. We had no destination, just a desire to "get out of dodge" for the day. We found a nice restaurant and had lunch and decided to go to the local mall for some shopping. Little did we know that we would come home with a very special package.

PetCo is a great place to find pet supplies and I was thrilled to step into this fabulous store and buy things for my animals. At the back of the store they were having an adopt-a-thon, so Mom, Deb and I wandered back there to see what animals they had for adoption. I wasn't looking to adopt a dog or cat, I had enough already, but heck, I had to take a look-see. Right?

In the back of the room, were all sorts of dogs, really cute puppies, labs, shepherds, and a tiny little doxie cross. Well, I asked to hold her. Mistake number one; never take a dog out to hold when you're not looking to adopt one. It didn't take long for me to realize that this little ball of fur was coming home with me. I knew that Michael would be ticked off like crazy, but I couldn't pass her up, she was just too cute and the ladies handling the adopt-a-thon said that she had come from an abusive situation. Sold! So I filled out the adoption papers and took her home with me.

She rode well in the car, and was the cutest little thing. We all took turns holding her and thinking of names. I liked Cheyenne, so when I called her by that name and her tail wagged, I said, "Cheyenne it shall be"

When Michael got home and was greeted by our menagerie of animals he at first didn't notice Cheyenne, but she came up and looked at him, then he looked at me. He was

41

none too pleased that I had adopted another animal. It was very tense around my house for about a month, but she was there and I wasn't going to return her.

It became apparent that Cheyenne had been abused. She was scared of the brush and would shake all over when I tried to brush her. She would scream when I clipped her nails and she would hide under the bed when Michael came into the room. I figured that a man had possibly hit her with a brush. I gave her rescue remedy and that helped to keep her calm. It was going to take time to get her comfortable with me grooming her, and even longer for her to trust Michael because he had a negative attitude towards her. Actually he was just miffed at me for not talking to him about getting another dog, and I knew I had been wrong in doing so, but I tend to do things on the spur of the moment and then think of the consequences after the fact.

Cheyenne was really a fun puppy. She and I went everywhere together. She became a perfect riding companion and would snuggle with my opossum Pocket in the car. She has gone on many long trips and is just an incredibly all around good dog. She is one of the best dogs I have ever adopted, despite her fears of being brushed. She is fiercely loyal and very affectionate and I do not regret bringing her home at all.

Michael began to warm up to her after a couple of months and now they are the best of friends. He has managed to find a way to brush her without trauma and trim her nails without her screaming. (*That is huge*) She snuggles with him and is the center of our family. She is now eight years old, the oldest of our adopted/rescue dogs, kind of the matriarch of the pack. Cheyenne enjoys spending her time lying in the driveway, watching the gate and barking to alert me of visitors, especially the moose, bear and deer that stop by occasionally.

Safia   Trisket   Cheyenne

Three of the precious dogs we have rescued. They love to peek through the fence post when we are moving the tractor, almost saying, "Hey, what about us, can we go for a ride?"

Chapter Three

Wonders of Nature
in your yard

"Those we have held in our arms for a little while, we hold in our hearts forever.

Anonymous

Bats in the barn roof

Summer in some states can be as hot as Hades with temperatures reaching well above 100 degrees. Construction workers often suffer mild to severe heat stroke and many take the brunt of the heat while working on roofs, especially tin roofs. Well, my husband was working on a roofing job, replacing shingles and he suffered more than heat stroke!

As the blistering tin roof panels were peeled off the dilapidated roof, the workers witnessed an eerie sight that scared many of them. The entire tin roof was filled with brown bats, hundreds of them, all sleeping quietly in the sanctuary of their "home." As the panels came off, bats fell to the ground and scurried off to find safe hiding places. That was OK for the adults, but the baby bats just fell to the ground helpless and vulnerable. Many of the workers "did away" with the babies, crushing them under their boots, saying they were a nuisance, unhealthy and that they carried rabies.

Michael tried to ignore the mayhem, but his conscious got the better of him and he went to the truck and got the cell phone. "Honey," he said, "I'm out here on this roofing job and, there are all of these baby bats and the guys are letting them die, what do you want to do?" "What?" I screamed, "Get them out of the heat and bring them home to me!" Clearing his throat he said "I knew you would say that, but Kari, you don't know anything about bats do you?" he questioned. "No, Michael I don't but by the time you get home I will, you have got to save them honey, please". He mumbled something I didn't understand and said he would bring them home. He was coming home early any way, he was feeling very bad and dizzy. I suspected he might be suffering from mild heat stroke and asked him to please drink some Gatorade. "I drank it all, but I still don't feel right, I'll be home in about an hour". "Michael" I said, "We'll get you fixed up and honey, I am so glad you called me".

As soon as I hung up the phone I got on the computer and looked up bat rescue. My heart was racing. Bats, how totally cool! I found very helpful information and printed it out, and then I called my network friends and asked if anyone had rescued bats. Two of them had and by the time Michael got home I had everything I needed to help the baby bats and to get Michael feeling better as well.

He walked in the front door; his face was deep crimson and blistered from the heat of the day. Although he was burned from the sun, his pallor was not good. I quickly got him some electrolyte solution and two aspirin. He headed off to the shower and said with a smile "look in my lunch bag." I had nearly forgotten about the bats, worrying about Michael. I rushed over and opened the bag, inside were tiny little bats, about two inches long, very dark, almost black in color, all huddled on top of each other. One by one I took them out and placed them in a large lidded shoe box with several layers of fleece. The babies quickly found hiding places. There were 11 in all, not nearly what I had expected. I was sickened to think of the poor little things being stepped on or roasting in the hot sun, but Michael had brought these babies home and at least, they would have a chance to survive.

By the time Michael was done with his shower I had prepared a mixture of kitten milk replacement formula with goats' milk for the babies and had taken unused foam make-up applicators and placed drops of formula on them. I took the babies out and watched as they suckled the tips like a nipple! I refilled the foam tips and they drank the formula, just like any mammal would. Their little feet holding on to each side, they were kneading as they suckled, just like a kitten. Soon their bellies were full and warm and I knew, just like with most infants, I would have to wipe their behinds with a warm damp cloth to get them to go to the bathroom. It's called stimulating them, I call it "pooping and peeing", my technical term. A heating pad on low was placed under the box. The babies were once again snuggled in their creases and folds of fleece, ready for sleep, or so I thought.

I washed up and changed my shirt and fixed dinner for us humans. We were sitting and talking when we heard a strange scratching sound. I couldn't tell where it was coming from, but soon my dog Cheyenne was sniffing by the table that held the bat box. They were awake! I had just fed them I thought and then I said out loud "they are nocturnal, of course, nighttime feedings, daytime sleeping, oh yippee." Michael looked puzzled as I talked to myself, but he was used to that by now with the rescues I had done. If I wasn't talking to them, I was thinking out loud. I finally went to bed around 4 AM. The little ones would eat and then sleep and wake, and play and eat, sleep etc. etc. It was fun to watch them milling about the box, touching noses and laying on each other. This was by far one of the most interesting rehabs I had done, I was very thankful to Michael for saving them. He just shook his head and said, "If I hadn't it would have haunted me." Good guy!

Three of the little ones died within two days of their rescue, but the rest thrived and progressed well during the next couple of weeks. They were getting bigger and more active at night. Their eyes were open and while I was cleaning one, the others would crawl up my arms and sit on my shoulders. Bats make a clicking noise when they are content (or so I have read). I would rub the top of their heads and they would click, kind of a baby cooing in bat language. After three weeks had passed they began test flying in the bathroom. I knew that they were ready to go to a colony and be integrated with others of their own kind, but where? We didn't have any bats at our place, so I made some discrete inquiries and our friends Sam and Patti, who lived on the river, had an old house on their property with an unused chimney that was full of brown bats! Problem solved.

We made plans to take the babies to their home in two

weeks. During that time they doubled in size and were being very naughty, flying all over, making my woodpecker Cousie go nuts and my dogs bark like crazy. I had a heck of a time gathering them up. They would fly just out of reach, clicking and then dip past me as if to say "he he he, you can't catch me!" Thankfully after I had gathered them up, I was able to leave food out for them at night, which was quite a blessing because, I may be a night owl but I am not a night bat!

The evening came when we went to our friend's house. We arrived around 5:00 PM and visited for a couple of hours. The sun was setting around 8:00 so we ate our dinner and then got ready to release them to the chimney colony. Just before sunset, Michael took a ladder and the box of babies and climbed on the roof. I so desperately wanted to go up with him, but at the time I was suffering from severe vertigo and couldn't. He peered inside the chimney and a large brown bat came up to check him out. "Whoa, this is cool, you should see this guy, and he's huge." Michael said. Soon several more bats came up and were wondering what was going on. "Open the box Michael" I said from below. "Ok, here goes." He opened the box and took the babies out. An amazing thing happened next. As he took each baby out, an adult bat came up and "escorted" the baby into the chimney. It was as if the older bats were saying, "welcome home, children."

When all the babies had been taken in, Michael came down from the roof. We sat outside and waited for dusk. Our friends brought out a bottle of wine to toast the momentous occasion and as we poured, the bats began flying. One by one they flew around the trees and down to the river. I had tears in my eyes thinking how flawless this rehab had been. How those precious little lives has been spared and now they had a chance to live and be free. All of a sudden I heard clicking. Bats flew close to my head, up and around and past my shoulders, dipping their wings. Our friends were freaked out a bit, but Michael and I sat there and took it all in, knowing yes, they were saying goodbye but also, thank you.

Barnabas taking a nap on my hand

Bats are in serious decline nearly everywhere. Worldwide there are almost a thousand different kinds of bats, which compromise nearly one fourth of all mammal species. Of the 43 species living in the US and Canada, nearly 40 percent are endangered or are candidates for such status. Bats are important to the environment; they eat mosquitoes that spread disease and consume other nuisance insects. As a way of encouraging the continuation of the species, many people have gone to "gothic gardening" including plants and bat houses for these special and helpful "creatures of the night."

While many people fear that they will get rabies from bats, there has not been a case of bat related rabies in over 70 years in the United States.

Sara

Bundled up, I went to replace birdseed in the feeders outside. It had been an exceptionally hard winter. In April the snow still clung to the ground, even as the sun shone brightly. Migratory birds flitted from tree to tree impatiently waiting as I filled the containers. I was surprised to see so many coming up close, but with the temperature hardly reaching above 25 degrees, I could understand. Filling the last feeder, I noticed something on the side of a tree. At first I thought it was a piece of bark that had separated but as I came closer I saw a tiny flying squirrel hanging on for dear life.

Gently I picked the squirrel from the tree with my snow-gloved hands. I could feel it shaking from the cold and its tiny frame was bone thin. I rushed inside and retrieved a small box, filled it with fleece and turned on an electric heating pad. As I placed the little squirrel inside the box, she held on to my glove and tried to nurse the tip of the finger. "Oh no" I said aloud. "Not a baby this early."

She nestled into the fleece and began to warm up. I gave her a small amount of electrolyte solution, which she took well. Soon she was asleep. This gave me time to call around and see if anyone had baby squirrels in yet and what their suggestions were. I had done some squirrel rescue years back and was successful, but never a flying squirrel and one so emaciated. After a few calls and some Internet research I made up a batch of milk replacement formula. The local wildlife rehabber said flying squirrels were rare up here and when they had been rescued they usually were too far-gone. She felt that most likely the little thing wouldn't survive the night. I knew she was probably right, but I had to do what I could to at least make her comfortable.

I fed her a formula of ½ electrolyte solution, ½ milk

replacement and gave it to her in small increments not to over feed her. She nursed the bottle and pooped on her own. I cleaned up her box and let her rest for a while. The very act of nursing seemed to wear her out and she almost collapsed into the soft fleece. Her temperature had come up to normal and her poop looked normal too, but she was extremely frail and weak. Every couple of hours I gave her partial feedings and she nursed. Usually you would see some sort of response after a couple of hours, but there was none with her. She would nurse, poop and fall back asleep.

Around 3:00 AM I got up to check on her. Her bed was nice and warm. She was alive but her body was very cold. I got a small hand towel and put it in the dryer to heat it up a bit and took her out of the box. She snuggled into the towel and nuzzled my hand as I stroked her head. I moved my chair close to the wood burning stove and kept her bundled up. Her eyes kept closing and I could feel her body growing cold again.

She looked up at me as I held her gently, slowly the light of life left her eyes and then, she was gone. I laid her back into the soft fleece and covered her up. I cried not only because she had died, but also because she had been born too early and I knew that the coming spring would bring a lot of heartache with babies struggling to survive after such a harsh winter.

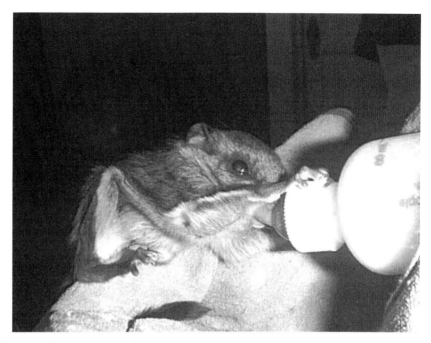

Sara, taking her bottle.

There is significant documented scientific evidence that our planet is experiencing a climate change, both naturally and also due to human exploitation. It is undeniable that animals, birds and plants are affected. Plants bloom earlier, birds lay eggs earlier and weather highs and lows, freak ice storms and drought can devastate and kill up to 1/4 of the offspring in one season, throwing nature severely out of balance and our animal friends in great peril.

We can do something to help. Plant vegetation that gives shelter, keep bird feeders full of seed and suet. Purchase or make birdhouses and keep them lined with pine needles or shredded newspaper. These simple things can help newborn animals have a fighting chance against the ravages of nature.

Oh Deer!

Living in the Pacific Northwest, we are blessed to be visited by many magnificent creatures: elk, moose, black bear, wolves, coyote, cougars and whitetail deer just to name a few.

One spring morning I was out milking my rescue goat Saffron, when I heard a rustling in the tall grass behind the barn. I finished milking and went out to take a look. The grass was about waist high and very thick, so at first I didn't see the little one lying there. My dog Cheyenne began barking at something and I looked over and saw a fawn. She was beautiful with a rusty red coat dotted with white spots gracefully caressing her small frame. I looked around for the doe and saw where she had been earlier; there was still blood on the ground where the fawn had been born. It was early enough that the doe should return, at least I hoped so. So with the dogs I went inside.

Despite my intense desire to go out every five minutes and check the fawn, I didn't. It took a great deal of self control not to, but I knew the doe would not come around if there was a human or dogs in the vicinity of her fawn. To use my time well, I got on the Internet and looked up facts on whitetail deer. I was pleased to see that often the mother would leave the newborn and go off to get food and return at dusk. With that information I waited impatiently for dusk.

Around 7 P.M. I went out to see if the doe had returned and if the fawn had left with her mom. She was still in the same spot as earlier in the morning. I put some deer food out for the doe and returned inside. I paced back and forth worrying. Just two nights prior we had a pack of coyote back behind the barn yipping like crazy. I couldn't bear to think that they might get hold of this precious baby, but I still waited until around 11 PM. With flashlight in hand I ventured out to past the barn and found the fawn was still there. "What do I do" I said looking at her. The fawn looked up at me and made a slight cry and I knew.

I went back inside and got a large bath towel. I opened the guest room door and moved the bed aside and put a tarp on the floor and covered the tarp with some large fleece. A fawn would not be a good inside rescue, but I wanted to monitor her for a couple of days and make sure she was strong enough, so I sacrificed the guestroom for the fawn. To rationalize this to my husband, I would tell him that we were planning on re-carpeting and re-modeling the room in a month, so how bad could it be, right?

I approached the fawn and gently picked her up. She didn't make a sound but looked at me and licked my face. My stomach twisted in knots and my heart tightened thinking of this beautiful baby I was rescuing. I was very thankful that I had fresh goat's milk to bottle feed her. One rescue helping another I thought as I carried the fawn inside. She took the bottle with no problem and drank half of the warm goat's milk. She was very fragile and not steady on her legs yet. Judging from her weight and size I surmised that she was maybe 24 hours old at the most. I cleaned her backside and made sure she pooped and peed and then she settled down into the fleece and went to sleep. I had placed a ticking clock near her to keep her calm. So far so good, I thought as I closed the door.

Around 2:30 AM I heard a ruckus in the guestroom. She was up and standing on the bed! Uh oh I thought, but was relieved she hadn't done anything except paw the comforter. I stood looking at her gentle face and smiled. "I think I will call you Ruby." At the time there was a song on the radio by the Kaiser Chiefs by that name, it was one of my favorite songs, so I gave her that name and went to warm a bottle of goat's milk.

She took the 2:30 A.M. feeding well and seemed to have more energy. I knew however, that she could NOT remain inside for much longer but that meant that I, or I should say Michael would need to adjust the goat barn to accommodate Ruby. I would try her in with our goat Saffron and see if that worked, but if not, we would have to make two runs and a separate stall for Ruby that was enclosed and safe from predators at night. That would mean taking the goats' barn and adding an apartment. "Oh, he will be thrilled when I tell him tomorrow" I mused. Poor Michael, just when he thought he had time to work on other things I would come home with some rescue and he would be building a flight aviary or something. This wasn't any different. He is very good at building and can make something out of nothing with little to no money spent, which when you do rescue is certainly a blessing. It's a lot of work and no pay, but it's worth it every time.

I got up around 6:30 A.M. and checked Ruby. She was sleeping but awoke when I came into the room. She jumped up and ran into me. I sat on the carpeted floor and took her tiny face in my hands. She licked my face and nosed me in the arm. I knew she was hungry so I stood up and walked to the door. I wasn't thinking and Ruby rushed past me into the living room. She hit the hardwood floor and sprawled flat on the floor. As she tried to get up she just kept slipping and my dogs were making too much noise. The barking and scraping of dogs and deer awakened Michael. "What in the__?!" he said. "She sneaked past me; I will get her back into the room and get her bottle, sorry honey." I said with a sheepish look. I tried to be quiet because Michael never gets to sleep in. "I do hope she is not going to be residing in the guest room for long," he said with "that" look on his face. "Oh no, honey, she is going out to the goat barn today, err, well if Saffron and she get along, that is". Michael stood looking at me and said, "Oh great, I know what that means; I have to build her a run, right?" I looked at him and smiled. "Yep!." He signed and I gave him a kiss on the cheek.

We went out and took Ruby to meet Saffron after the goat had eaten. It didn't go well. Saffron was very aggressive and knocked Ruby down several times. I did not want her to hurt the little fawn, so I picked Ruby up and took her back inside until we could get a run ready for her. Michael dug out some wire fencing and measured the stall and began work on turning a one-stall barn into a duplex, so to speak. He worked all day on the barn and by dark it was ready. I took Ruby out and gave her a bottle in her new home. She sniffed and walked around. We had placed a heat lamp inside and there was thick straw on the ground for her to sleep on. I stayed outside with her for several hours to make sure she was ok and ventured in around 9:00 PM. I was exhausted and Michael was already fast asleep on the couch. I looked at him and was thankful that he helped me with rescues like he did. Even though he would have rather spent the day working on our boat, he made a safe and warm space for Ruby.

Weeks went by and Ruby grew strong. The fresh goats' milk was excellent for her and she was thriving. I introduced alfalfa to her and she would nibble at it. I gathered brush from the property that the other deer ate and gave that to her as well. I even added Gerber baby rice to her bottle as an extra boost. I had done that with baby goats and they were extremely healthy and fit. I knew she needed to start running and that it was time for me to transfer her to my friend Gina. She did fawn rescue and had a 20 acre fenced parcel and within that a five-acre secure area for them to run and play and, Gina had two other fawns there as well. I gave her a call and she said she would come the following day and pick Ruby up. Her space was a perfect set up for Ruby to grow and do what deer do: run, frolic and play.

Gina showed up around noon, just after I had finished cleaning up Ruby. Even though I knew it was best for Ruby to be with other deer, my insides just hurt. I didn't want to give her up because I was afraid that when she got older she might get shot by a hunter or hit by a car, but I also knew that it was not my place to keep her as a pet. She deserved to be free. With tears in my eyes I helped Gina load her into the back seat of her truck. I kissed Ruby and she licked my face. I gave Gina four gallons of fresh goats' milk and some alfalfa. "Kari, it's going to be OK. Come over and see her whenever you want to, you will love to see her play with the others." Gina reassured me. "I know she will be OK. I just have never been around a fawn before, and they are so loving and tender hearted. I feel I have learned so much from her gentleness and having her has made me more aware of that in me." Gina looked at me and said "I know exactly what you mean."

Over the months I stayed in touch with Gina and went to see Ruby a couple of times. She was running with her playmates on the five wooded acres. One of Gina's older rescues was now a doe and had taken the three orphans as her own. She was very attentive to them and it made me feel so good to see them all safe, well adjusted and thriving in such a beautiful place.

The following spring Gina let the yearlings out to the rest of her property to meet and be with the other deer. There was a rather large herd that stayed on the 20 acres so it was only natural to let the yearlings be out and among their own kind, yet in a safe environment.

Ruby comes back to the five acres now with her own offspring. She is very healthy, with a nice coat of fur, though she is now somewhat wild. Ruby still doesn't venture off Gina's 20 acres, which we are grateful for. Ruby seems very content to be living out her life in harmony with nature, without the threat of being hunted.

Ruby, as I found her in the tall grass.

The whitetail deer are one of the most graceful animals in the wild. Their body length is up to six feet and they stand about four feet tall at the shoulder. Their diet consists mostly of fruits, nuts, berries, grasses and twigs. They can reach a speed of up to 30 miles per hour and reach an age of 15 years in the wild.

Rascally Raccoon

My friend Ellie is a rescuer, too. We met several years ago and have shared some rescue animals. It's kind of a joint custody thing. She will have the animal for a week and then I take it. This works out well so that we don't get too burnt out. Such is the case with Roxie.

Ellie had received a call that an orphan raccoon had been found. She picked her up and began taking care of her. The problem is, Ellie has two boys that are, to put it mildly, quite a handful, so Roxie being a baby took a lot of time and Ellie needed help. Enter Auntie Kari! She called me up and sweetly asked if I wanted to care for a baby raccoon. Uh yeah! I love raccoons. They are such characters, like little mischievous gremlins.

Roxie was darling. She loved being held, took her bottle easily and was just the most perfect and delightful little bundle of trouble you can imagine. We would have our playtime and I had to be on guard like mad because Roxie would get into trouble in an instant. For example, I was on the phone giving someone advise on a bird they had found, I turned around and discovered Roxie had torn up a pillow off my couch. She was sitting on the floor with stuffing all around her just throwing it up in the air. I could almost hear her saying "whee" as she played with the cotton. I didn't get mad. Actually I laughed hard and went over to her, picked up the mess, gathered Roxie in my arms and gave her a kiss. I am not a tough love kind of gal.

After a feeding, I would run a warm bath in the tub and set Roxie down to play. This solved two problems, the first being that I didn't have to poop and pee her and the second, she would be occupied for a bit, which, was great because a baby raccoon requires a lot of time and energy. They love to play and are quite demanding of your attention. Roxie had a bunch of toys that she would splash around in the tub. She loved blocks and would stack them on top of each other and then swipe her paw and strew them all over the tub. It was so cute to watch. She was VERY smart and very obnoxious as well.

As Roxie grew she became more demanding and began to get aggressive. She gained weight and would run behind me, grab my pant leg and scurry up my back to sit on my shoulder. Her paws were amazing, like little human hands. She would touch my face, pull out my earrings and play with my hair. If I set her down and put her in her cage, she would scream. I knew that the time was coming to begin letting her get wild so that she could be released. Ellie and I talked about it and she wanted to take Roxie back to get her wild. I was all for that and we made plans to meet and I would bring the little terror back to Ellie. Roxie had torn up books, magazines, pulled spices out of my cabinet in the kitchen, destroyed rolls of toilet paper and basically made a shambles of my house while she was visiting. I had forgotten how destructive a raccoon can be, and was more than ready to let Ellie have her back.

Far off the beaten path sits Ellie's country home. National Forest is directly behind her five-acre parcel. She had a huge fenced enclosure to put Roxie in, with a tree in the center and stumps for her to play on and burrow in. There were berry bushes also, so Roxie could begin foraging for her food. This would also give Roxie a chance to catch and eat bugs and be outside, where she needed to be.

I was holding Roxie as we opened the door to the enclosure. She didn't want to let go at first and held on to me like her life depended on it. Her sharp claws dug into my shoulder as I gently pulled her away and set her down in the grass. She ran and scrambled up my back and began pulling my hair. It really hurt! I knew she was frightened, so I sat down inside the enclosure and brought the young raccoon into my lap. Ellie sat next to me and within a few minutes Roxie began to notice things in the grass. She leapt off me and began chasing bugs. And then she found the tree! She was up it like a shot. Ellie and I left her in the enclosure and went inside. We watched Roxie from the kitchen window; she as having a ball playing in the tree and running around. The weather was warm and she would have no problem acclimating to her new surroundings.

A few weeks later I received a call from Ellie. She said that Roxie had been getting very wild and she could no longer pick her up. That was very good news! It meant that our efforts of rehabbing her had been a success and she had not become imprinted. Many mammals and birds that are rescued will become so tame that they cannot be released back into the wild. They are unafraid of humans, so that for their own safety, they need to be kept out of harm's way. That is called imprinting. They take on the characteristics of the rescuer and cannot survive alone. Raccoons on the other hand, will get wild when put outside and left alone. It is a survival instinct and is quite amazing to see.

Ellie had opened the enclosure. Roxie had begun exploring the property. She would venture off and return at night for food and water. Within a month, Roxie had found a male raccoon her age and brought him over for food. They would scamper off all day and get into untold mischief. It was perfect. Ellie began moving the food farther away from her house, and off into the National Forest property. Roxie would eat and leave, and eventually she didn't come for days and then weeks.

It has been a couple of years since we shared the rescue of Roxie. Ellie still sees her from time to time in the trees far off her property. Roxie has babies of her own that sit and look down at Ellie from a huge tree. It's heartwarming to know that we were able to give Roxie one more chance and that she is healthy, frolicking and back in the wild, where all wild things need to be.

Roxie, enjoying bathtub playtime

Roxie (lower left), and her new family

Raccoons may weigh up to 35 pounds. They are nocturnal and remain active most of the year. During the winter months they live in their dens and live off food storage of body-fat. If weather permits, they will forage for food during winter months. Their food consists of nuts, berries, fruit, crops, mice, fish, frogs and crustaceans. If water is available to a raccoon they will dip their food into to it as if cleaning it. Actually they take in water by using their "hands." Raccoons may live in the wild up to 15 years of age.

Chapter Four

Opossums, opossums everywhere!

*"Living with animals can be a wonderful experience,
especially if we choose to learn the valuable lessons animals
teach through their natural enthusiasm, grace, resourcefulness,
affection and forgiveness.*

Richard H Pitcairn

The Doctors Office

4:33 AM the phone rang. Jolted from my sleep I fumbled for the phone to catch it before it rang again, waking my husband. "Hello?" I half mumbled. "Kari, this is Diane. I'm so sorry to call you this early but I need your help and I need it now." "Diane" I whined, "Its 4:30 AM, you know I am allergic to mornings." She chuckled and said "I know but the cleaning crew at the doctor's office came in and found what appears to be a dead opossum, with babies suckling."

Instantly I jumped up. "OK, I'll be there in five minutes" I said as I started running around my bedroom with the phone under my chin. "Thanks, kid I owe you" she said and hung up the phone.

Diane was a terrific lady. She had started the network many years prior to me joining and had been one of the first women on the coast to get a 501 © 3 in place. She took classes and slowly a garage-based rescue turned into a network of hundreds of people across the country, each with specialties doing their best for the benefit of animals. Diane was on hiatus for a while; she had finished a rough go with chemotherapy and was still quite weak. But that didn't stop her from being in the middle of each rescue! I was looking forward to having her back 100% and was thankful that she was feeling strong enough to stay involved.

Scrambling for clothes, I pulled from the pile next to my bed; jeans, sweatshirt, socks and hiking boots. I rushed into the bathroom and quickly re-braided my hair, topping it off with my Animal Rescue cap. My emergency rescue bag was ready and I grabbed a large plastic garbage bag and a small box with soft fleece as bedding, ready for baby kits. I threw everything into the car and paused to jot a brief note to Michael. "Gone to rescue possums, be back??? X.O."

Driving with a million thoughts in my head, I took in the silence. The streets were still as night clung to the sky; I rushed to the medical building. Looking for a place to park I mused, funny thing, vacant streets in this coastal town allow NO Parking from 3-6 AM. Frustrated I went around the block and found the cleaning staff entrance and zoomed in, throwing my rescue bag and gloves into the baby box. I rushed to the back entrance. A worker met me at the door. "Senorita, come quick, Paco is about to take a broom to those ratons." I was terrified and almost screamed, "NO senior, por favor, tell him it's OK, please!"

The worker ran down the hall and we were just in time to stop Paco from killing two of the newborn opossums with a push broom. I rushed past him and swiftly picked up and gently placed them in a box. "Is that all of them?" I asked. "No, no, senorita, there are more running all over the place". Oh great I thought, "OK, tell your men to move slowly and let me know when they see one. I need to get them into this warm box right away. Where is the mother?" I asked. The poor worker seemed dazed by my orders and questions, but I knew if the mother was dead; the kits could die from suckling her. It was a matter of urgency.

As we walked down the hallway I put on my leather gloves. "My name is Juan" he said as we reached the end of the hallway. I introduced myself and smiled. He pointed to a slightly open door and showed me where she lay. Gently, I reached out to touch her, placing a towel over her head. I took out my stethoscope and listened for any signs of life. Her body had blood on it and it was cool to the touch. "She is dead, no, senorita?" he asked. "No, Juan, actually she is not dead, she is injured and playing possum". He stood looking at me and I knew he didn't understand what I was saying. I figured in his opinion this was one big ugly rat!

"Ayeeee!" a scream came from the hall. "We found the ratons!" someone frantically yelled. "Ok, let me cover her and show me where they are". Around the corner a frightened cleaning woman stood pointing. There, huddled around a dust mop were five baby opossum. Saying a silent "thank you" to God that they were all right, I reached down and picked them up one by one. They seemed fine, just scared and cold. As I passed her the scared woman made the sign of the cross. I had to smile. "Juan, I need some hot water," I asked. "It's over here." He showed me to a small sink and I took some surgical gloves out of my bag and filled them with warm water. Tying them off, I placed them in the box with the kits. Their instinct kicked in and they all crawled around and on top the warm gloves and soon fell asleep.

Juan and I walked back to where the mother lay. Gently I gathered her up and placed her in a towel I had knotted at both ends. She was injured, extremely thin and seemed very old. All I could do was keep her warm until I got home. I took two more gloves and filled them with warm water and tucked them next to her. She had not moved at all. I thought she must be dead, but I carried her to my car and placed the towel into a large box. As I went back inside, the workers thanked me for coming. They seemed relieved and yet a bit sad. I picked up the box with the sleeping little ones and peeked inside, they were snuggled up nice and warm in and around the gloves. "Adios, Amigos" I said. "Gracias".

Driving out of the parkway garage daylight had begun to slowly bring life to a new day. "Life as usual" I thought as I passed a street sweeper. Then as I turned to head home, I wondered, would this rescue save all of the lives and bring them a new day? I would have to wait and see.

Rescued kits cuddle up on a warm surgical glove

Opossum are the only nocturnal marsupial of North America. They raise their young in a brood pouch like a Kangaroo and they roam and forage for food at night. They can have up to 15 kits per littler ranging in size from ½ to 5/8 inches long when born.

The mother licks a trail from her vulva to the brood pouch and the newborn kits travel up and into the pouch where they attach themselves to one of the 13 teats. Not all kits survive. They will live in the brood pouch for several weeks and then venture out and ride on their mothers back until old enough to go out on their own. While it is said that an opossum kit will ride on the tail of its mother, that is untrue.

The Fatal Bite

The sun crested the hill just as I drove into my driveway. Spider webs glistened with scented dew and bees began their labors of the day. I took the box with the injured mother opossum and made my way into the house. Michael came out of the front door ready for work. "Hi Honey, I waited for you, but I am running late. Man, you look beat" he said. "Yeah," I sighed. "What's in the box?" he asked, concerned. "I have a possum in bad shape and another box with seven hungry babies, I've got to get the mom stable and try and save her, if I can, but it doesn't look good." He kissed me on the cheek and said, "I wish I could stay. I'll call you later, ok?" I looked at him and half smiled and asked "What time is it anyway?" "Time for me to go to work" he quipped. "Love you." I mumbled, "Love you too" as I carried the box inside with the injured mom.

What seemed like many hours had only been one hour since I had gotten the call from Diane. It was now 5:48 AM. I took the mom and placed the box on my makeshift "triage" table then went outside to get the babies from the car. In my garage I had a rescue hospital of sorts and I transferred the babies into a small dog carrier on a heating pad. They were moving around looking for momma, but that would have to wait. Momma needed help now.

I sat at the table and took off my gloves. Rubbing my hands together I said aloud, "OK Momma let's see what's going on with you." Slowly I removed the towel from the box and placed her on a remade babies changing table that adequately served as my exam table. The top was covered with a foam pad that I had covered in vinyl for easy cleaning and the shelves underneath held medical supplies and other items to treat an injured animal. I grabbed my baby scale and weighed her. She was terribly thin, emaciated by wildlife rehab standards. She had not moved at all. Lifting her up in the towel, I replaced the scale on the shelf. Gently I laid her on the foam pad and slowly unwrapped the towel from her head. Wham! In an instant she lunged at me, biting my middle finger almost clear to the bone. "Holy Toledo, that hurts!" I said to her. She crouched on her side and growled at me. My finger was throbbing and bleeding and I was wondering what to do now. I had to evaluate her, but didn't want to be bitten again.

Never handle an injured animal without leather gloves! I had been told this a million times. That statement pounded through my head in time with my finger as I realized the predicament I was in. I would have to report the bite to Animal Control. Dang, I had been so foolish. But, foolish or not I had an injured animal that needed help. Quickly I poured betadine on my finger and wrapped it in gauze. Tucking the end in, I put my leather glove on. I used a wrapped towel as a barricade to keep her yellowed gnarled teeth from my hands. I proceeded to give the old girl the once over. She was about seven to eight years old. That was the oldest momma opossum I had ever seen.

Her pelvic area seemed dislocated and the blood appeared to have come from an angry wound on her back that looked like a bite. I suspected dog or coyote. Not good for her, or me! She was covered in fleas and very pale. Quickly I cleaned her wound with betadine solution. She growled from behind the towel and I moved as fast as I could, gooping triple antibiotic into the wound. That would have to do for now. I dusted her for fleas and gently moved her legs. She growled and hissed at me again. I went to the frig and got out some amoxicillin and gave her a shot for the infection. She watched me with cautious eyes as I worked fast, trying not to hurt her any more than necessary. When I had finished, I put her in a medium dog carrier in the "hospital". I gave her some soaked dog kibbles and yogurt with some fresh water. She didn't move as I covered her cage.

Peeking in on the babies I saw that they were moving around looking very hungry and lonely. I got down a stuffed toy and put it inside with them while I went to fix their food. I warmed fresh goats' milk and formula and then set about feeding them one at a time. Soon their bellies were round and warm and each one had done their "business." They snuggled together by the stuffed toy and nestled down for a nap.

My finger was very swollen and hurting like mad. I washed it with veterinary betadine again and treated it with triple antibiotic. Laughing out loud I said "Hey, if it's good enough for her, it's good enough for me'. Unfortunately, I knew I needed to file a report with Animal Control, but I put that off and got my intake paperwork out and filled in all of the pertinent information about the animals. Yawning, I looked at the clock; it was nearing 8:00 AM. I decided that I needed to take a little nap. It had been one heck of a morning.

The phone rang at 10:30 A.M. I reached over to answer it and my finger began throbbing again, a not so subtle reminder of the earlier events. Diane was on the other end asking about the opossums. I filled her in and told her about getting bit, she was a little angry with me and instructed me to report it today and asked if I was up on my tetanus shots, which of course I was. I thanked her and hung up the phone.

First things first, I needed to check on the opossums. The babies were milling about wanting food. I took out the soiled bedding and put a fresh piece of fleece in. After about half an hour I had fed them, helped them do their business and they were ready to take another nap. These little babies will do fine and will be able to be released back into nature, I thought to myself. I was so thankful to see how strong they were. Their momma, even though she was old gave them a good start. Momma, oh yes, I need to check on you, dear lady, I thought. I moved the towel covering the front of her carrier and she was lying in the back, very still. She didn't look at me and her head was at an odd angle. I grabbed my gloves and

71

reached in. A cold chill came over me as I touched her. She was dead.

On no! What had she died from? I was scared because I knew now I *had* to call Animal Control immediately and not only report a bite, but also report that the animal that bit me had died. I dialed the number and spoke with Officer Ramirez. Being a rehabber I was always talking with one of the officers about injured birds or mammals and they all knew me well and thank goodness, respected the work I did for the animals. He said he would be right over; he was just down the street.

In about five minutes he knocked on my front door. Looking very stern and concerned he asked to see the dead opossum. I took him to her and he placed her in a specimen bag. He made notes and asked me a lot of questions. Ramirez chastised me for not calling immediately. "You know the rules Kari, any animal bite has to be reported when it happens and we have to fill out a report." "You are not immune to that responsibility, you know, just because you have had your rabies and hepatitis vaccinations." I was really getting worried, thinking I would get a fine, or that they would take away my permit to rehab, when all of a sudden he broke out laughing! "Man, I need to remember not to let you bite me! She bit you and now she is dead, you killed her Kari!" Ha-ha! I found no humor at that moment. In fact, I didn't think it was funny at all, but he reminded me, "Opossums don't carry rabies remember, she looks old, we'll run some tests, but I am sure it's nothing serious." He tried to make me feel better but started laughing again as he put the poor dead opossum in his truck. "Wait till they hear this back at the office." He drove off laughing so hard he had tears in his eyes.

As a side note, the tests came back negative. The opossum had died from old age and emaciation. Her approximate age was 7-8 years of age. Opossum may live in the wild up to 8 years.

An Opossum named Pocket

Having an opossum for a pet was never my intention. When she came in as a baby, I treated her like any other rescue, but Pocket was different.

From the very beginning Pocket wanted to be held and would spend her time sitting on my shoulder, nuzzling my ear. She loved to be rubbed on her belly and after feeding she would poop in her litter box, clean herself up and scratch at her carrier door to get out. She didn't keep normal opossum hours either. If I was up, so was Pocket. Opossums are nocturnal, they find dark places to rest during the light of day and make their way out at night, all except Pocket! She loved the light and she loved me.

My little friend Pocket, as a kit

When I got Pocket, she was s single orphan with no siblings so my thought was that she would quickly become part of the litter and fit right in. Nope! When I tried to put her in with the others, she would have nothing to do with them, wouldn't eat and hung on the side of the cage, waiting for me. It broke my heart to see this little thing pining away like she did, so I took her out and decided that we would make the best of each other.

A few friends at the network had pet opossum, and we talked about keeping them, after a few phone calls I realized that if she was happy, why not? I can tell you; this little girl was such a delight and was sweet and loving. Yes, I know, they look like an overgrown rat, but they are very clean and affectionate when they feel safe. Pocket was all of that and more. We became inseparable and while I was doing housework or on the phone, my little friend was there with me. I would take her out on rescue calls with me too. She loved to ride in the car and was a perfect little lady sitting on my shoulder watching as cars went by.

Most of my friends were into rescue, so to see an opossum sitting in the car was nothing. But to my other friends, well, they freaked. Most of the time, I would hear an "OMG" followed by a scream. "For goodness sakes, it's just a baby opossum," I would say. That usually didn't make any difference. To the average person these guys are road kill or garbage scavengers, not cute fuzzy snuggle babies like my Pocket! Boy, did they miss out on a good friend.

She grew up and got bigger and even though she wanted to sit on my shoulder, she was too heavy and her long tail would wrap in front of my eyes, which made for hazardous driving. The last time she was on my shoulder in the car, a man looked at me and then his mouth opened, he swerved and I thought he was going to cause an accident; luckily he pulled over and got his wits about him. I had to chuckle at it, but I realized that she had overgrown her baby seat on my shoulder, so I had to find a new place for her in the car. Eventually she got used to the small dog carrier and would sit there quietly as long as I scratched her nose while I was driving.

When she was fully grown her nocturnal instincts kicked in and she preferred to stay at home and await my arrival at dinnertime. I would come in, let the dogs out, check messages and get Pocket out of her apartment. Then we would spend time playing. She would sit on the little rescue table and eat her raspberry yogurt with a few grapes on top and watch me make meals for the rest of my rescue critters. Pocket liked to run in the backyard and would follow me around. She never tried to run away and would only stay outside while I was there. She liked to dig for bugs while I was feeding the owls, crows, hawks and other animals in rehab. My dogs didn't bother her either. Cheyenne, my rescued Doxie-cross, would sniff her and lick her nose. It was really sweet to see such a happy family of mis-matched critters all sharing space in such a loving manner.

When Michael and I had to move to Montana I was shattered to leave my babies, especially Pocket. I felt like I was abandoning her and the other animals I had taken in, but we had no choice. My friend, Jeff, who had several opossum, told me that she wouldn't make it in Montana because of the cold weather, even if she were inside. Opossum are prone to pneumonia in a normal climate and with the severe winters it would surely mean death for my little friend. The night before we had to leave I took Pocket out and we watched TV together for a couple of hours. She rested on my lap and licked my hand. I brushed her and kissed her nose and cried silent tears knowing this would be the next to the last time I would hold my little Pocket.

The next day as Marilyn arrived to load up the crows and the two opossum, I reluctantly entrusted Pocket to her for safekeeping. Little Boy was fine; he seemed to take to Marilyn with no problem. But Pocket clung to me for dear life. She knew that something was up and she didn't like it. I held her one last time and hugged her, and then I took her paws from my neck and placed her in Marilyn's arms and ran inside sobbing. I couldn't believe that my heart could break so deeply over a critter that most people would just shoot. Even now, as I write these words, the memory of her comes back and my heart feels the loss all over again.

Pocket has a good home with Marilyn and has adjusted to her new life. She is spoiled and loved and had a litter of kits the year after she went to live with Marilyn. I am grateful that she is happy, but my heart has an empty space that cannot be filled because; there will never be another Pocket.

Pocket, all grown up and beautiful

Chapter Five

Take these broken wings

"The sky is round and I have heard the earth is round like a ball, and so are the stars. The wind, in its greatest power whirls. Birds make their nests in circles, for theirs is the same religion as ours.

Black Elk, Oglala Sioux Holy Man

The Swallows of the University

Every collage campus prides itself on pristine gardens, well-manicured lawns and nicely groomed trees and of course, clean buildings. With spring-cleaning in full swing, the university workers noticed that a huge nest of swallows had been knocked down. They quickly gathered the birds and placed them, along with with the contents of their broken nest, into a box and called the wildlife rescue. We agreed to take them and made room for what we thought were a few. One of our rescue ladies had been sent to pick up the birds and was not prepared for what she found. There were 37 swallows, of all ages in this box and, there was also another box. The tree trimmers had accidentally knocked the mud nests from the building and made homeless over 70 mud swallows! Our little rescue facility had just a few incubators, which already were full of babies. This was going to be a group effort if these birds were going to survive.

When the rescuer arrived back at the center we began separating the hatchlings from the fledglings and so on. "If we don't get everyone involved, this is going to be a nightmare." she said. We doubled up other birds and made makeshift incubators from anything we could find. Using what was left of their nests, we placed tissue inside and put the tiniest of the birds back into their familiar nests, and then we put them in the incubators. Taking count we had 73 swallows. Our little group worked for hours stabilizing the birds, mending broken wings and calling rehabbers to take the older bird's home.

We placed about 20 by six o'clock that evening and made a schedule of who would come and feed the others during the next two to four weeks. "I'll take the injured ones home with me" I said. "Great, Kari, they might not make it you know"... I knew that but agreed anyway. I had pretty good success with injured birds and felt that I could give them more intensive care. I took 9 home with me and was on schedule to help at the center each day from noon until three, seven days a week.

Diligently each volunteer came and did their time, feeding, cleaning and helping these homeless birds survive. I lost several in the first few days from injury and trauma and then we would lose one or two every other day for about a week. But as the weeks progressed we made great progress, the birds got stronger and eventually the tiny but mighty network of volunteers had saved over 60 of them. It was teamwork that saved those birds, each of us doing what we did best and helping out as needed. We never quarreled or spoke out of turn; we just jumped in and gave 100% to save the birds. Each of us was given the pleasure of releasing our charges and so we all took them back to the University, to rejoin the rest of the swallows in the area.

Six of the nine I took survived and had a second chance at life. I was amazed as I released them, that they took to the sky so fast and furious and joined their kin. Their little faces seemed to smile as they sped into welcome and familiar territory. This is what rescue is all about, I thought.

Baby swallows as they came in, featherless

"We're ready to go home now"

Wa'ipi Kwinaa (Woman Bird)

To a Native American, all animals are sacred. Each is revered for its gift to the earth and the strength that gift brings to each of us, if only we would understand how to receive it. Many, who are struggling to find their way back to nature and to our Mother, have found solace in their Native American heritage and ever so slowly are walking in beauty upon the Earth.

California, a melting pot of culture, is not without its share of Native Americans. Many have relocated from reservations to the gentle climate that this state offers and many are indigenous to the land itself, having been born on reservations in the southern part of the state.

During the spring you can find many pow wows to attend, with all tribes dancing and celebrating their heritage and the sacredness of our Mother Earth. It is at one of these that I came upon a Shoshone man, Patrick, who after being introduced to me by my Oglala friend Peter as, the "bird lady", became very insistent that I help him with a bird he had rescued only that morning. "I was walking just as the sun rose and I heard a cry, not from the clouds, but close to the ground. I stood in silence and listened and followed the cry. It was only a few yards away from where I stood, a Wa'ipi Kwinaa, a female hawk was injured. Her wing is broken." Patrick explained. I stood looking into his dark eyes and could see the compassion he felt for this bird. As we talked I was reminded that hawks are sacred and was told that this hawk would need to be released back to where it was found and I would need to allow he and the others from his tribe to assist with the rehab of the bird.

That was going to be a challenge for many reasons. First, I was a woman, second, not from his tribe and third; I was unfamiliar with the protocol in dealing with elders from any tribe. It was a bit unnerving to think of this task, but I knew that everything happens for a reason and there was a reason behind this rescue. "Patrick, where is the bird now." I asked. "I have her at my place; I could bring her here to you if you like." He suggested. I felt that was the best idea. Patrick was in a grass dancer competition that day so we agreed to wait until after the pow wow and I would take the bird. "I caught a mouse today, in the field and she ate it" he told me. "Patrick, that is a good start. If she is eating then she has a good chance at recovery. We just need to get that wing looked at right away," I said. He acknowledged with a nod and walked back to his tent to get ready to dance. I grabbed my cell phone and called Dr. Beth, the rehab vet, and told her I would be bringing in a hawk with a suspected broken wing. She was on the night shift at the vet hospital so it was okay for me to bring the hawk in on my way home, or so I thought.

Later in the day Patrick disappeared. I assumed that he was with some of his friends, but soon he appeared with a box and inside was the hawk. She was a beauty, a red-shouldered hawk with juvenile feathers. "I called my vet and she is ready for me to bring her in this evening to check the wing" I said. "I will take her now and call you with the results of the exam" Patrick looked at me and said "No, I will go with you. I want to meet this vet and explain that the bird must go back to where I found it". "Patrick, she knows that." I urged. Sternly he said, "You don't understand, this is my responsibility, Wa'ipi Kwinaa called out to me and I have to make sure that everything is done right". I knew there was no arguing with him. I just didn't know how Beth would take it with me walking in with a hawk and Patrick!

We loaded her into my car and he followed me to Beth's office. I had tried to call her on the way but my cell battery was dead. It was about an hour drive from the grounds where Patrick and I had met, and I had a lot of time to think as I drove. This was not a regular rescue. I knew that I had a responsibility to not only the bird, but to a culture as well. I was not unfamiliar with native culture as my grandfather was Cherokee and I had danced at pow wows for several years, but I was not deep into the culture. This adventure would open the door to many new experiences, I suspected.

Beth was a darling plump pregnant blonde with big blue eyes. She looked all of twelve years old, if a day. She stood in the doorway as we walked up the stairs to the hospital. Patrick looked at her and then at me, his eyes wide. I could see he was not pleased with what he saw, "I need to talk to you Kari." he said. We set the box down and walked out the door. I looked back at Beth who stood there puzzled to say the least. "This woman is a child; I don't think this will work." I stood looking at him, so regal in his appearance yet, he was naïve, like a child. "Hey, she looks really young but she is a fantastic vet and has helped me with many birds. She is one of the only vets that knows anything about raptors Patrick, trust me, she will do what is right for this bird". He stood looking at me and took a deep breath. "I was told that you are the bird lady, so I trust you, but I don't know her". We discussed the bird and the vet and finally I told him "Look, she is it. I can wrap the wing but I can't x-ray it with my eyes. I am sure this bird is going to need more than just a wrap on her wing Patrick." He stood looking at me and said, Ok, but you keep her with you, and she does not stay here." I agreed and we went back in to see what Beth could find out about the injured hawk.

After careful examination and an x-ray, it was apparent that her wing was broken and she was very malnourished. Beth set the wing in a very different manner than I was accustomed to. "Kari this fracture is such that this wing must be completely stabilized. We might have to put a pin in, if it doesn't heal properly, then you know rehab for this bird would be months." Dr Beth said. With that prognosis, she gave me some fluids to tube her with. I was good at tubing raptors and had the equipment at my home. I had gotten over being bit and clawed. It usually happened anyway. It was just part of rescuing a raptor with talons!

Patrick and I walked outside; he carried Wa'ipi Kwinaa to my car. I looked at the compassion in his dark soulful eyes. "We will need to stay in touch during the healing of her and when she is ready to fly, I will bring you to my *res* and you can meet the elders and be part of the ceremony." I smiled at him and nodded, though I was uncomfortable about meeting elders. I was not as familiar as I should be with customs, especially of the Shoshone! We exchanged phone numbers and Patrick said he would make sure I had enough food for the bird. "That's not really necessary, I have raptor food in my freezer and get a constant supply from the Wildlife Network I volunteer with" I said. "I want to be involved in the healing of this bird and I can offer you help with food and you can teach me some of what you know". He almost pleaded. "OK, sure, here is my address. Why don't you call me in a couple of days and you can come over and I will show you what I do." Patrick smiled. It was the first time I had seen him smile. He was so stoic and regal, but the smile softened his chiseled features.

Six weeks passed and Patrick and I worked with the bird. She was healing well and getting feisty. Dr Beth had X-rayed her again and the break had mended. We were able to remove the wrap and allow her to stretch her wing. Patrick and I took Wa'ipi into the flight aviary in my backyard and watched as she ran the 100-foot length and then all of sudden she flew to the perch! "Wow that was amazing!" I exclaimed. Patrick looked at her and then at me. "You are the bird lady, aren't you?" He asked. "Well, I have been working with them for a long time and to be honest, I feel that they are a part of me." I said with a smile.

She was left in the aviary for two weeks to gain flying strength. Patrick brought live mice over for her to hunt. She was incredibly beautiful as she would swoop down and snatch the mouse in her powerful talons. She was ready to be released.

I called Patrick and told him that she was ready and that it would be great to do it the upcoming weekend. "You will bring her to the *res* and meet the elders on Saturday" he stated. "Uh, ok" I stammered. Not knowing what I should do, I called my friend Peter and told him what was happening and asked him for advice as to what I should do on Saturday.

Peter's father had been one of the last Sun Dancers in Rose Bud South Dakota, a very powerful Sioux elder and Peter had taken over where his father had left off when he passed on. "Be respectful; wear your ribbon shirt and the feathers I gave you, in your hair. This is a ceremony of life. The elders will ask the Great Spirit to protect the hawk and all who are at the ceremony," Peter said gently. "This will bring you closer to the spirit of the animals you rescue, and will connect you more with Mother Earth, Kari." I respected Peter and humbly thanked him.

On Saturday I drove to the *res* and was met by Patrick and what seemed to be an entire tribe of his people. Most were wearing their regalia. I was excited and scared at the same time. Slowly I got out of my car and opened the back door to take Wa'ipi out. Patrick motioned me to a large group of elders. I was asked to sit. I sat down with the box containing the hawk in my lap. The drums started and people slowly stood and began moving in a circle. Patrick began dancing in time with the drum. My heart was beating so fast that I felt like I would pass out. An elder motioned me to stand and bring the box to the center of the circle. I was shaking. Patrick kept dancing round and round; the colors of his regalia echoed the many colors of grass blowing with the wind. The drums seemed louder and I gently opened the box when the elder instructed me to. With a gloved hand I took Wa'ipi Kwinaa out. Everyone stood in the circle gazing at the magnificent hawk. She looked around and flapped her graceful wings to the beat of the drum. The elder motioned Patrick to stand beside me and nodded to me and then, I let her go.

She flew up and around, her wings still beating in time with the drums. She let out a 'kree' sound and flew back closer to us and dipped her wing. And as quickly as she came down, she flew off into the clouds. I was invited to dance in celebration of the release of this hawk. As I danced to the beat of the drums, tears rolled down my cheeks. I kept looking upward and could see her darting in and out of the clouds. At that moment I felt my heart soar with her into the sky.

Of all of the rehabs I have done, this was by far the most spiritual experience. I not only was I involved in the rehab of an incredible raptor, but I met and was embraced by a very proud tribe. My respect of these people has deepened and my self-awareness of my own native blood has given me new insight into walking in beauty and being a vital part of Mother Earth.

Wa'ipi in the aviary

Panic on the Pier

Cheyenne and I had gone for a nice long walk on the pier in Santa Barbara and were enjoying the sounds of the waves crashing along the pier posts. We would take long walks each day to either the beach or the pier and meet interesting people along the way.

This particular day we heard a terrible commotion at the end of the pier, a couple of young boys had been fishing and their hook had caught the wing of a brown pelican. People were running and panicking not knowing what to do. In my fanny pack I had a Swiss army knife, making my way down the pier I knew that the bird needed to be freed before the hook ripped his wing to pieces. I tied Cheyenne to a bench and hurried over to help bring the pelican in. He was a majestic beauty. The young boys were scared, and the pelican was thrashing about, attached to the fishing line, but they had it on the pier, not still flying in the air, which was a blessing.

I rushed over and gently grasped the wings of the pelican; his strong beak pierced my arm and I winced in pain. I found the hook site and snipped the fishing line. The hook had penetrated into the shaft of one of his feathers but it was not bleeding. Quickly I removed the hook and let him go. He nailed me again with his beak and then took to the railing. I knew he was partially in shock and most likely was hurting, but he didn't fly away. He sat there looking at all of us. I was concerned and then I noticed a pail piled full of freshly caught fish. He wanted a fish!

One of the boys took a fish out and threw it at the pelican; he opened his huge beak and swallowed it whole. After a few more fish he decided to take to the sky and dive into the ocean. The panic had faded and people resumed their normal strolls along the pier. An old man patted me on the back and gave me a toothless smile as I went to untie Cheyenne.

As Cheyenne and I continued our stroll along the pier the pelican landed on the railing accompanied by two sea gulls. It was such a beautiful sight. I marveled, knowing that just a few minutes prior this endangered bird was caught and might have lost his wing, or died. I took my camera out and snapped a photo as a reminder of this special bird, and of this special day.

It's amazing, you can be anywhere and if you are observant and pay attention, you might be able to save a life. I am always on the lookout for things that are not normal where wildlife is concerned and I have been fortunate to be at the right place at the right time.

Brown pelicans are facing the possible extinction of their species due to environmental issues such as oil spills, pollution and being caught in fishing lines off piers. It is estimated that an average of over 1,000 birds get caught up in lines each year and many tragically drown because of fishing hooks tearing their beak pouch.

Gregory

I'm a girlie girl I admit it! I tend to overdress for parties and I never leave the house without my make-up. For years I would faithfully go and have a manicure to make sure my hands and nails were presentable. Ha, such a waste of money for a rehabber!

Sutchi was just finishing up with my manicure when my cell phone rang. Gingerly, I picked it up and answered. It was the network and there was a Great Horned Owl that needed rescuing immediately. The problem was, it was on the side of a steep embankment and I most likely would have to scale down on a rope to get the bird. I wrote down the details, told them I would be there within a half hour and hung up the phone. I sat in the chair thinking for a moment. I was wearing a silky summer dress and pretty sandals and had a lunch appointment with my friend Caroline. So much for my $35 manicure and, adios to my lunch!

Opening my trunk I pulled out my rescue bag and grabbed a pair of jeans, a long sleeved shirt, thick socks and hiking boots. I went back into the salon and changed in their restroom. I pulled my hair pack into a ponytail and donned my rescue cap. I was ready to find this raptor.

My mom always liked to come with me when I went out on a rescue, so I called her and said I would be by to pick her up in a few minutes. Mom asked me all sorts of questions when she got into the car, mostly, "you're going to do what?" I explained to her that I might have to use a rope to get the bird. She of course was upset, but she knew that I would do it no matter what she said. I have a stubborn streak in me and I am fiercely independent.

We arrived at the location. I pulled out my binoculars and perused the embankment. It was very steep with lots of brambles and at the base was a creek that rushed past. I spotted the owl about one quarter of the way down. He was beautiful and majestic. But, I knew that there was a serious problem. He was sitting still, in the middle of the day, in plain view. Something was very wrong with him and I had to get to him ASAP.

He was about 100 feet from me. I hooked the rope to my bumper and put on my gloves. Tying the rope around me, I gathered my net and gave the rescue box to mom to hold. "Kari, you're not going down there?" she asked with a quiver in her voice. "Mom, this is what I do and yes there is no other way to get that bird." Slowly I inched my way down. It was wet and very slippery. The brambles caught my shirt and scratched my face. There were water ticks on the rock and soon all over my shirt. My stomach tightened as I tried to brush them off me, to no avail.

As I made my way down the embankment I saw the owl. He was just sitting on a rock. It appeared that he couldn't fly; it looked as if his wing was badly broken but he was quick and kept moving further away from me. I was nearly at the end of my rope, literally, when I took a chance and extended my net over him. He was awkward and thrashing inside the net. I quickly began pulling myself up the wet rock. Mom was standing looking down at me; I could see she was scared to death that I would fall. To be honest, so was I. If I slipped it would be the end of the owl, and me.

Mom grabbed the rope and tried to pull me up. I kept slipping on the wet rock and almost lost the net as I grabbed at some brambles to steady myself. My entire body was shaking. I was soaked and covered in water ticks. With a burst of strength I pulled myself up and over and hauled the owl over with me. I began brushing the ticks off me and took a deep breath to help ease the queasiness that gripped my stomach.

With trembling hands Mom handed me the box. I opened the net and gently took out the owl. His keel was sharp and his wing broken, but he was fierce and struck me instantly with his talon, embedding itself into my thigh. He kept tightening his grip and the pain was almost unbearable. I slid my right hand down and grabbed his talon. He relaxed for a second and I dislodged the razor sharp talon from my thigh. I quickly put him in the box and sat on the ground. "You are never doing this again" Mom scolded. I looked at her and smiled. "Next time I won't tell you" I quipped. She didn't find that amusing at all.

We loaded up and headed back to my house. Mom came with me as I brought the owl in. He was beautiful and after I weighed him, I knew that he had been without food for several days. The average weight of a Great Horned Owl is 2 to 5 pounds. He weighed only 1.8 pounds. I took a frozen mouse from my freezer and thawed it out. Usually a rehabber has about a dozen or more mice that are frozen for food, on hand at all times. I opened the stomach of the mouse and sprinkled some Vita Hawk into it. I hoped the owl would eat the mouse so that I wouldn't have to tube him, but he did not. I had wrapped his wing. After giving him a thorough examination it was not as badly broken as I had first suspected.

I warmed up the raptor formula and tested it on my arm, just like baby formula. The temperature was right so I filled my syringe with it and attached the thin tube to the end. Slowly reaching in the box I took out the owl. I wrapped him in a towel and placed him on my lap. Gently I opened his beak with my gloved hand and inserted the tube down his throat, making sure not to get it into his breathing passage. Within a few minutes I had given him 5 cc's of formula. Nothing came back up when I removed the tube to which I was greatly pleased. Tubing can be very dangerous and if any fluid gets into the lungs the bird will aspirate and die, usually within 24 hours. I am exceedingly careful NOT to let that happen! I un-wrapped him and placed him back into the box. Silently I said a prayer. "Please let him live and let me do what is right for this bird."

The owl was a difficult patient. He was in pain and being wild, did not like my poking and prodding. But the formula helped him stabilize and within four days he was eating mice and chicks on his own. His weight came back and his wing healed well. He gained two pounds, which was excellent progress. I put him in the flight aviary after a week of R&R and after just two days he was flying and catching live mice. It was such a relief to see this magnificent bird doing so well.

The owl was extremely aggressive. When I would enter the aviary he would fly at me, talons first. I wore safety goggles, a leather jacket, leather hat and gloves. He nailed me a couple of times but only nicked the arm of my jacket. Had I not worn protective clothing, I would have had serious injuries. I let him hunt for another week to gain strength and weight.

I called Mom and told her it was time to release the owl. She drove over and we loaded him in the box, but not until he had finished two mice with vitamins. I wanted him to leave with an extra boost.

It was nearing dusk and we drove to the area where I had rescued him. I took the box out of the car and opened it. He ran out and took to the skies, his massive wings elegantly pulling him higher. The feather structure of a Great Horned Owl is such that they make no noise when then fly. He silently circled and then landed in a large oak tree. I took my binoculars out and looked up the tree; there was a huge nest further up the tree. He flew from the branch and circled again and this time landed next to the nest. My heart leapt as I saw what appeared to be his mate, come out. She was much larger than he and just as magnificent. This was very exciting to see as mating season was nearing. It was the perfect ending to this rescue. I had the owl for just a little over a month and he had gone from starving to thriving. Owls mate for life and he was given one more chance to be with his mate for the remainder of his natural life.

Gregory just before he was released

The Great Horned Owl, one of the largest of all owls does not have horns, but tufts of feathers that stick upright.

With a wingspan of five feet, they utilize silent flight that comes from fringed flight feathers that muffle sound. They hunt from above and behind and their prey never sees or hears them coming. A great Horned Owl can live up to 20 years in a protected environment, but only between 5-15 years in the wild due to accidental poisoning and loss of habitat.

Willow

Being known as the "bird lady" has its up's and downs. I usually never have any down time when it comes to bird rescues. Just as I release one, it seems that there are two more to take its place. I barely have time to clean cages before I am inundated with more birds.

The network had received a call about an unusual bird and no one could identify what it was. I had just come from a visit to a bird museum and had bought all sorts of books on identifying birds. So, I went down to check the bird out and see if I could help identify it. The bird was brown, with spots all over the very soft feathers. The mouth was extremely large and the coloring suggested that it was a nightjar, which was an uncommon sight amongst rehabbers. Nightjars are a close cousin to the swift or swallow, and shares titles with the Por-Wil of the south. It uses its wide mouth to catch flying insects thus being an insectivore.

A couple that had been replacing their front steps had brought in the bird. The bird was under the steps and when they removed the wood, the startled bird flew into their window and knocked itself out. He also had tweaked feathers and they thought it might have a broken wing. I asked if I could take it home and treat it, and everyone was more than happy to let me have it, because no one knew what to do with a bird like this. Actually I didn't either but I had books, the Internet and an instinctual second sense in healing birds, so I put the brown bird in a box and headed home.

I pulled out my new *Encyclopedia of Birds* and found the chapter on nightjars and frogmouths. It was fascinating. The birds are indigenous to almost the entire world but are rarely seen. Their feather coloring is a perfect camouflage for them and they blend in with tree stumps, rocks and foliage. Nightjars are superbly equipped to capture insects on the wing at night. A nightjar can engulf large numbers of mosquitoes in a single snap or wheel about and sweep up a Luna moth. Because they have only a four-inch wingspan, this makes for some tight and fancy flying. It is said that these birds can echolocate. That means that they emit sounds that allow them to avoid collisions with trees while foraging at night. They are truly one of God's most fascinating birds.

I named my new charge Willow and went about gathering moths and other flying insects to feed him. He ate mealworms, moths and mosquitoes. I had a light on at night and gathered as many as I could to feed Willow. He was not sitting upright when I brought him home, so I gave him some Hypericum for a couple of days. He righted within no time and I could see no reason to keep him. I had been feeding him for over a week and he seemed to be eating rather well, though he disliked me putting things in his mouth. He began making strange noises at night and I felt that his time had come to go home. I was prepared to take him out and document his release with pictures but Willow had other ideas.

I went to his cage to feed him and he shot past me so fast that I fell to the ground. He flew up and over the fence and disappeared into the night. There was no sight of him and no sound either. He just became absorbed by the darkness.

That was the only Nightjar that has ever come to the network. I have since read more on them and they are quite uncommon as rescue birds. The Hopi Indians have a folk tale that these birds hibernate within rock crevices. The Hopi call them "holchko- "the sleeping one".

Willow, the illusive Nightjar

Chapter Six

Sad Tails, Happy Endings

"If you have men who will exclude any of God's creatures from the shelter of compassion and pity, you will have men who will deal likewise with their fellow men.

St. Francis of Assisi

Angie

For over a year a loveable blue tick coonhound sat at the shelter awaiting a forever home. Her owner could no longer keep her and gave her up. Plus she had a disadvantage, an insatiable desire to jump and climb fences, making her a challenge to adopt. Weeks passed, soon turning into months and still Angie was not adopted. During the first few months of Angie's stay, people fell in love with her *mere cat* eyes and sweet disposition, but her inability to stay in a fenced yard kept her from finding that forever home.

She became attached and very protective of me because I was the kennel manager and was with her seven days a week. She would growl at anyone coming into the kennel area and she just kept climbing fences. I felt helpless, as did the other volunteers at the shelter, thinking Angie would be a permanent fixture and possibly unadoptable.

Then one day a lovely lady named Carol came in and went right over to Angie's kennel. Angie growled a bit and then began wagging her tail. Within a few minutes Carol asked if she could take Angie out for a walk. With a big smile, I said "Yes, please do" and handed her a choke collar and sturdy leash. "She can be a bit hard to handle sometimes," I told Carol. She looked at me and said "It's OK, we will be fine." Carol walked her for well over an hour and came back with a tentative smile. "I think I will take her."

At the shelter meeting later that evening, I sat fidgeting in my seat waiting to tell everyone the good news. "Angie got adopted," I blurted out of turn. Silence fell over the room. "Yep, Angie got adopted today; the lady is coming in tomorrow to pick her up, isn't that wonderful?" We all cheered and I thanked God that Angie had found a good home with such a lovely lady.

Carol picked Angie up the following day and promptly took her to PetSmart so that she could pick out toys. All of the volunteers at the shelter thought that was terrific that this woman already had decided to make this a partnership with her new friend. Angie was enrolled in obedience training that very day. (Not that she needed it).

She finished intermediate training with flying colors. Carol proudly said that Angie would run through the doors of PetSmart and look for her classmates; she was fond of a Mini Pin and two Standard Poodles, whom she romped and played with after class. "Angie is the perfect companion; she is a good helper, good company and a good partner for me. I am thrilled to have her in my life and I love her dearly" beamed Carol. Angie went on a six-month vacation to Texas with her new mom in a motor home. Carol sent us a note telling us how perfect this adoption had worked out. "I feel safe and know that she will protect me and love me and most of all, keep me company."

Even dogs with challenges can find forever homes. It just takes time and patience, a lot of love and of course, the right person.

Huckleberry Jazzmean:
The Kitten from Hades

My sister and I decided to take the day and venture into Trout Creek. This tiny little town in Montana is host to the Huckleberry Festival, a three-day event celebrating the small, tart and much prized fruit, the huckleberry. Usually the weather is hot and muggy but that doesn't keep people from streaming in from all over. This festival is attended by thousands of people from over four states.

Making our way into the parking area, we sat sweltering in the hot sun, windows open, sun block on our baking arms. It was nearing noon and the temperature was close to 95 degrees! Outside the car I noticed a miniature dachshund skirting between cars, carrying something small and alive in its mouth. We were at a standstill, so I put the car in park, jumped out and took out after the dog. A log truck nearly squished the tiny dog as it inched in the line of cars. The dog turned and saw me and dropped its mouthful. I saw the black mass move- it was a kitten!

Frantically, I grasped the kitten in my hands and moved as another log truck lumbered past. Thank God, I thought. As I looked at the tiny little kitten in my hands, a cold chill ran inside of me, it was still wet with sticky blood clinging to its fur; it had just been born. Even though it was 95 outside the kitten was cold and shaking. I ran back to my car and told Deb, "We have to find where this kitten came from." Looking at me Deb realized that our day of fun would be a day of rescue.

Deb pointed to a ram-shackled singlewide mobile home. "I think the dog came from over there." We moved the car out of the snail's pace line, parked and went in search of the mother cat or more kittens. What we found was disturbing and so needless. A brick fire pit had old papers half burned on top and lying in and amongst them were 3 newly born kittens, covered with ants! They were cold to the touch and we knew if we didn't pick them up they would surely die. We looked for the mother cat and found her dead halfway under part of the deserted mobile home, blood everywhere and a still born kitten in her birthing canal. She was so tiny, just a little over a kitten herself. It made my stomach turn. We looked for something to bury her with and ended up covering her with old bricks.

We wrapped the kittens in a towel from my small rescue bag and Deb began brushing the ants from them. Their unopened newborn eyes streamed tears as the ants bit and burned their tiny flesh. We sat in silence as I drove the 15 miles home. The kittens were hungry and cold. Deb held them in her arms and rubbed them gently. As I glanced over at the kittens I knew that they didn't stand much of a chance at survival and the stark reality of feral cats struck home, again. It appeared that whoever had lived in the mobile home had left in a hurry, leaving behind possessions, and cats. Unfortunately for the abandoned cats, the result was inbreeding, heatstroke, dehydration, starvation and ultimately death.

I pulled into my driveway and we quickly took the kittens out. We got them into a nice warm shoebox with fleece, on a heating blanket. I warmed kitten milk replacement, added some Colostrum to the mixture and filled miniature bottles. Kittens need Colostrum from their mother to give them a boost and also the immunities that the mother has in her system as well to survive. They were reluctant to take the nipple at first and were very weak. With gentle coaxing they slowly began to suckle. We wiped their behinds and made sure they pooped and peed and placed them back into the box.

Deb took the kittens to her house to rehab as I was caring for bats and had taken a job. We talked about the fact that they might not all survive, but she agreed to take them and began the process of rehabilitating the babies. The first day they all seemed to be doing ok. She gave them their formula every couple of hours. The following day, one of the kittens had died and another had serious diarrhea. The formula was not being digested and as soon as it was fed, it would shoot out. We tried several remedies for the diarrhea including small amounts of corn syrup but nothing worked and the kitten died the following day, leaving only two.

The rescue was heartbreaking to Deb as she tried to save the kittens. But after around 15 days, two were getting bigger, eating and moving around their bed. She had placed a pocket watch under their blanket to stimulate the sound of the mother's heartbeat. One morning Deb went in to feed them and another had died. She was devastated and called me. "I don't want to do this anymore Kari, they are all dying". I tried to reassure her, but knew that if any survived it would be a miracle. "Keep trying Deb" was all I could say.

The sole survivor was a totally black kitten who when it nursed moved its ears back and forth, Deb called it "Spock". It seemed stronger, larger than the others had been and each day took the bottle and grew. Within 2 weeks Spock's eyes began to open and he was trying to stand. He was odd looking with a really large head and a skinny body. It was a struggle for him to hold his head up, but daily he did get stronger and began to fill in. We were elated that Spock had come along so well. Deb had done a great job with him, but was ready to say goodbye. She got a good job that required her to be focused and get good rest so she couldn't take the time to do nightly feedings any longer, and Spock was not taking solid food yet.

I had released the bats and took Spock in for the rest of his rehab. He grew and got feisty and one morning while I was cleaning his backside I realized that Spock was a girl! I changed the name to Jasmine but quickly changed that to "Jazz-mean," as this kitten was mean! Definitely a feral kitten, she clawed, scratched, bit and hissed at everything. She would hide for days and attack the dogs. I was not sure what to do because this was the first truly feral kitten I had ever had and this one was a handful of 'meanness'. My other rescue cat, Maile, was super sweet and Jazzmean would attack her at every opportunity.

Within six months it was time to get Jazz spayed and, oh-my-goodness, the poor vet tech! When I came to pick her up, I was greeted by the bandaged tech whose hands were torn to shreds along with her arms and neck. It seems Jazzmean decided that she didn't like the tech and lunged at her, bit her neck, found any exposed flesh and literally began tearing her up. The only thing I could do was to apologize and offer to pay for any medical bills; she was such a sweet gal and just said, "It's all in a day's work." I knew about getting thrashed by raptors, but a cat, wow! I was shocked and deeply concerned that this black ball of evil would be living with my tame and spoiled pets and that she could do them great harm especially my newly rescued pug puppy and my Woodpecker Cousie. I placed her in the carrier, but not before she bit my hand and raked her claws over my exposed arm.

As Jazzmean began to mature she slowly became less aggressive, however she would still lurk around corners and attack anything that moved. She hung on pant legs, the base of a broom, chased the vacuum, rode on the back of our old dog Lucy and was just an unholy terror. My lovely new curtains were torn from top to bottom in about an hour, the mini-blinds sat askew in the windows. I placed all my trinkets in boxes to prevent the systematic breaking of them, as she was prone to do. I had a hard time with the destruction of my house because even though I have animals, I keep it very clean and always ready for company. We toyed with the idea of making her an outside cat, but the hawks, owls, coyotes and bears made that impossible. And there was some creep in town that was poisoning all the cats that were not inside. We were stuck with the 'Kitten from Hell', whether we liked it or not!

Jazzmean would let us pet her after about a year, without removing a bloody stump. Michael could pick her up for 30 seconds or so and then, wham; she would whack him in the face. He wasn't too keen on our new addition to the household, but tolerated her. When we moved to Idaho she seemed to take the ride well and loved the new house. She had stairs to run up and down and could leap at everything. Shortly after we moved, two tiny feral kittens found their way into my garage and I brought them in the house and began feeding them. Surprisingly, Jazzmean didn't mind them and seemed to know not to harm them. She played gently with them as they grew. They have grown into terrific cats, with no feral issues.

That was four years ago and now Jazzmean is a wonderful cat. She has her perch on top of the small refrigerator, loves her toys and sleeps at the bottom of the bed. She doesn't bother the birds at all, never did. Her best buddy is my husband, Michael. At night they have a ritual, he gets into bed, she comes to his side of the bed and makes a "meep, meep" sound, and she then in turn will get on the bed and "kritch" or make biscuits as most people call the pawing movement. She's a kick. Is she still a terror? You betcha! She is like lightening up and down the stairs, but my trinkets are no longer of interest to her, she prefers the new imported Chinese rug in the dining room to play in, under and around!

The kitten from Hades

Jazzmean, the terror of the Thompson's

Chi's in need

Just pick up a newspaper and there are hundreds of ads for puppies with price tags that can reach well over $1000. The new thing is mixed breeds that carry hefty price tags as well. There are Pom-chis, Chugs, Labradoodles, German Shuskies, Austra-healer-weiners and the list goes on and on.

Movies can play an interesting if not predominate role in the breeding of dogs. Kids see a dog in a popular film and they want one. It's a case of demand versus supply. Enter the puppy mills. Now, don't get me wrong, there are reputable breeders out there; one of my closest friends breeds Champion Show Long-Haired Doxies. She is very careful with her breeding and she also does home inspections to make sure her purebred puppy goes to a proper home. That sadly is not the case with many breeders.

When a movie has come and gone, the dogs remain. And the cute puppies are now adults, with little to no hope of an adoptive family, so they sit in cages often three to four high in rooms. After the Chihuahua movies came out, everyone had them for sale, darling teacup chi's with big eyes and frail little bodies. Many got adopted but as it is with any fad, very few of the humans did research on the breed and the breeders just wanted to get rid of their plethora of puppies. Chihuahua's especially, are not for everyone. They are very fragile and can become injured easily; they are yappy, bite and are basically a one-person dog.

While I was at the rescue shelter an elderly woman came in asking if we could place 11 of her older chi's. We had no room for them and tiny dogs do not do well at a shelter anyway. The stress element is too extreme and they suffer from the many traumas associated with kennel life. A friend of mine was visiting me at the time and said she would take them in to foster. I was thrilled because Terri already had rescued several chi's and they were happy and well adjusted. She was the perfect solution to the problem presenting itself. Terri took six of them. Before she left the shelter we filled out the paperwork, took pictures of the dogs and got their vaccination records from the lady who brought them in.

This left five unclaimed chi's. I got the doggie *Wish List* out and began calling everyone I could find, asking if they would like to adopt a Chihuahua. The answers saddened me. Most had already bought from a breeder and many of them wanted to place the dogs they had purchased because they weren't what they expected. My call ended up with a new list of four more chi's in need of homes.

We placed the remaining dogs in foster homes and ran ads in the local newspaper offering them for adoption. They went quickly, which was surprising, but the people interested in the little dogs were older, had previous experience with a Chihuahua and wanted a lap companion. Terri did a fantastic job in finding homes for the six she was fostering and eventually kept one for herself. Not too long after we had placed the dogs, the same lady came back in with more. These were even older than the first batch and had been kept in kennels most of their lives. They weren't as easy to place.

Terri took one named PJ. She had an eye problem that the lady had been treating with an antibiotic ointment. Terri called me and asked for a voucher to take her to the vet to be checked. I agreed and the results from the vet's tests were not positive. Her eye needed to be removed and the cost would be around $500. Our shelter didn't have that kind of money and had an outstanding bill at the vet awaiting payment. After I explained this to Terri she said she would pay for it herself, providing we reimburse her. I took her proposal to our Board and everyone agreed to get the dog's eye fixed and that we would pay her back.

The surgery was a success and PJ was feeling better without the ulcerated eye. She was given a good bill of health from our vet and we were told that she was around eight years old. She still had a bit of playfulness in her and enjoyed being held, so she would be an excellent candidate for adoption, providing her eye grossed no one out.

It didn't take Terri long to find a home for PJ. She met a very sweet 65-year old lady who had just lost her faithful companion of 14 years and was very eager to give another dog a special home. When Terri took PJ to visit, tears filled the woman's eyes and she held PJ close. "I would love to give her a warm and loving home for the rest of her days, if you will let me," she asked Terri. The woman didn't mind that she was missing an eye and Terri called me with the news. It was a fantastic new beginning for PJ, and another successful adoption of these chis's in need.

Little Chi's who found forever homes

PJ, after her eye surgery. She is loved and cared for in a special home with a lovely lady

For the Love of Lucy

Several years ago, my Mother was renting a house from a, shall we say, testosterone infused macho man named Arturo. Now, don't get me wrong, he was pleasant and a very good landlord, but he had a sadistic streak in him when it came to his dog, a corgi mix he called Lucy. Arturo would leave for trips to Europe and show up at mom's house, literally throw the dog out of the car and say, "I'll be back in a month". Poor Lucy would look after him with sad eyes as he drove away. It broke my heart to see how Arturo treated Lucy. He had started dating a woman who had a young dog and he no longer had time for Lucy. Arturo said she was an old dog and he was planning on taking her out to run "one last time" and then shoot her! Well, I would have none of that, nor would Mom, so we pleaded with him to give us Lucy. Finally he agreed and we took her in.

Lucy had been roughly handled and she was a geriatric dog. From what we could surmise after a visit to our veterinarian, she was about 13, almost blind in one eye and was beginning to show signs of hip dysplasia. Despite her disadvantages, Lucy enjoyed running and playing in my large backyard, and was a very affectionate dog.

Having a dog that had been mistreated was not unfamiliar to me, but knowing the person that did the mistreating made it even more difficult. Lucy was timid and head shy, but she would run and get in the car to go for a ride at a moment's notice. Often I would open the car door and Lucy would jump in, look up at me and settle in for a ride. I hadn't really needed another dog, but she was no trouble at all and the affection shown to her was, in my mind, payment for a life of abuse.

Lucy enjoyed five years of cuddles, good food, gentle care and all the human affection Michael and I could muster.

She never lacked for anything as she began to slow down. And when her hips began giving out, she was treated to the best veterinary care, along with glucosamine to make her comfortable and pain free for as long as possible.

When she was 18, she had become very disabled and could barely move without help. One of the hardest decisions I had to make was to put her down. Her quality of life was no longer good. Lucy was suffering and I couldn't bear that for her. She had suffered at the hands of a cruel man, and she would not suffer any longer. I wept over the loss of my friend Lucy, but I knew that she had been given another five years, of happiness, and even in her last moments she knew that she had been loved.

Our sweet old Lucy

Chapter Seven

Imprinting and Education Animals

"The difference between friends and pets is that friends we allow into our company, pets we allow into our solitude"

Robert Brault

On Education Birds

First let me applaud anyone who has the knowledge to care for education birds or any bird for that matter. More often than not, they have been injured and cannot be released back to nature. The educator has the responsibility of providing a healthy, stress free environment in which the bird's can live. This includes the care and feeding of the bird's, not to mention vet bills and transportation. This is a 24/7 dedication to lives. And many raptors can live up to 25 years in captivity. That is a serious commitment.

Educators bring nature into classrooms. They inspire young children to do right by animals and often inspire them to volunteer their time to help animals as well. Most do not charge for their presentations. They do it for the love of the birds that we coexist with. They do it because most humans don't really know a lot about raptors or wild birds. For most, the experience of something wild is usually seen on *Animal Planet* or in a movie.

We need educators to continue to present programs to our youth. We need rehabbers to care for injured animals and we need rescuers to bring them to safety. It's a finely woven web of help and love, of caring and devotion to nature and all that belongs in nature. These people, who dedicate most of their lives, are the few, not the many, but their contribution to our planet and our animals is invaluable. Let us bless the teachers, for they open the minds of children, who are *our* tomorrow.

The Rat Pack Crows

One of the most delightful rehabs that I had the
privilege of assisting in was that of baby crows, 27 to be exact.

In the spring when baby birds hatch and have
feathered, they begin exploring their surroundings.
Unfortunately many fall out of their nests. Good Samaritans,
will pick up a bird and take it to an animal rescue office. More
often than not, if the bird is left alone, the parents of the
fledgling will continue feeding the baby until it can fly,
provided it doesn't get attacked by a cat, dog, raccoon, or for
that matter, a mean kid.

At the Wildlife Network, spring was our busiest time.
We had baskets of baby birds of all kinds from hummingbirds
to robins and almost every kind in between. We had bunches
of baby crows and most of the rehabbers didn't like to deal
with them because they are very messy and stinky. Now I, on
the other hand, love corvids. For most of my adult life, ravens,
crows, jays, magpies and all of the others that make up this
dynamic species have fascinated me. They are extremely
smart, very playful and are amazing to watch as they mature.
The Network had three ladies who would rehab crows but they
were so burnt out over the last couple of years that they asked
for time off. I volunteered to take in baby crows when they
came into the network. *What a job!*

The first chore was to make an environment for them
with perches and wire to enclose them. Michael and I had
made an enclosure that was approximately 10 feet long by four
feet wide and three feet tall. We used shade cloth attached to a
wooden frame on the sides and top. This worked well, or so
we thought until some critter got into the enclosure and killed
four fledglings. I was devastated when I went out in the
morning to see them torn to pieces. Michael and I re-thought

the enclosure and came up with a very sturdy living environment made of thin gage wire with a plywood top.

At the time of the attack I had seven fledgling crows in our first enclosure. Now, there were three and they were suffering from injuries sustained from the attack. Each crow was treated with antibiotics for any possible infection, their wounds were dressed daily and they were given Rescue Remedy. Handling them constantly was not the best thing to do for them, as they became very tame and imprinted. An imprinted bird is one that feels safe in the company of humans and ultimately cannot be released. We made a separate enclosure for the imprinted crows when a huge batch of new babies came in. I named the three imprints, Sammy, Frankie and Dino: The Rat Pack Crows. Frankie still had blue eyes and was thin as a reed, Sammy was blind and Dino had equilibrium issues. They got along well, and even with their physical difficulties, they thrived. However, after just a short while, we knew these three would not be able to be released.

The new group of twenty-three babies was very healthy and my days were spent feeding them. At the break of dawn they would start calling. I would go out with formula in hand and start at the left side of their enclosure, by the time I had made it to the right side; the babies on the left were hungry again. This went on until dusk. They were doing well and getting big. Now I understand why most people want to pass on crow rehab, they have insatiable appetites!

As they grew and began eating on their own, I placed them in the flight aviary. I could not believe what a mess they made in just a couple of days. Food was everywhere, poop on the sides of the walls and the smell… it was not pretty. They are darling despite their messiness and I was so pleased that we have saved 23 of them.

Michael had added a release door to the flight aviary for them and after six weeks we opened the release door and one by one they flew out. I thought they would take off and be gone, but no, they wanted to stay with Momma Kari in her nice backyard! Our neighbors were none too thrilled when they saw 23 crows in our huge oak tree. And when I came outside with food, the noise they made was, well, very loud. Slowly they began to move on and eventually we only had a few that stayed around, mainly for the food and, well, they were lazy (very unlike a crow).

The Rat Pack Crows grew and even with their disabilities they thrived. Frankie loved to be held and would cuddle up with me at night. Sammy was rather distant, but still would let me hold him and rub his chest; though he died of pneumonia complication during the second year we had him. Dino eventually righted himself with the aid of Hypericum and rescue remedy.

When Michael and I moved to Montana, my friend Marilyn took them and they went to a really awesome home. I still receive emails from her telling me about their antics and what a pleasure they are. She takes them to schools with other birds and educates kids on the importance of respecting nature and being kind to animals.

Two Rat Pack Crows, Frankie and Dino

When Corvids *gather it is called a* Murder of Crows, *or a* Conspiracy of Ravens. *The* Corvid *consists of crows, ravens, jay's, magpies, jackdaws, rooks and nutcrackers.*

Many people fear the Corvid, *as a harbinger of death. But many Native American tribes revere these "tricksters". A raven or crow may live up to 25 years in the wild and are incredibly smart, which aids in their longevity.*

Tyto

Captive breeding of migratory birds and raptors in the United States is not permitted, however in Europe there are many breeders who legally sell their birds to falconers. Occasionally, there will be someone who "finds" a baby raptor and decides to make it a pet. Such is the story of Tyto.

Tyto was "found" by Jane who thought she could raise a barn owl, though she had no experience with them, nor did she have a place to keep one. Shortly it was discovered that Tyto was a lot of work and I was called to take her and see if indeed she was imprinted and to give her the proper food, housing, etc.

Tyto was tame, which was not good. She was very young, with tufts of down still clinging to her delicate legs and chest. She was loveable and liked to sit on my lap, walk down to my knee and watch television. When I would put her in her cage at night she would scream like mad, so for a time she had the run of our guest bedroom. Tyto was extremely smart and learned quickly. She would get off the bed or chair, go to her paper and poop and then come back. I was sure she was hopelessly imprinted and Jane, who found her, really wanted her that way. This bothered me. The woman didn't have a barn owl, so in her mind it was ok to keep Tyto tame and easy to handle and she knew that I would be the right person to keep her that way. My reputation as a loving, successful rehabber preceded me, but that also was one of my selling points as a rehabber, I was always given birds that were in trauma.

I began an experiment. I would work with Tyto and encourage her to be an owl, not a pet or a toy. I began teaching her to hunt in the aviary. At first she would have no part of it, but then she began liking the chase. Soon, she was swooping down on a mouse and flying to a perch to devour it. We were making great progress except that she would not stay in the aviary at night.

I phoned a falconer friend in England for help. He had been a falconer for over 30 years and also bred birds for fellow raptor enthusiasts. He suggested that I let Tyto stay in the aviary during the day without me. She screeched like mad. It was unnerving to hear the sounds she made. She would fly to the window and peer out at me, screeching. It just broke my heart but at the same time, I knew that this is what needed to be done so that she could be free and not a captive show bird.

It took about two weeks to get her to calm down, but eventually she did. I would enter the aviary; bring her live mice and leave. She would hunt, fly and roost, which was terrific progress. Jane came over to see how "tame" Tyto was and expressed shock to see her in the aviary. "What have you done? That was supposed to be my bird!" she screamed at me. Holding my tongue, I took a deep breath and explained that although Tyto was tame as a baby, she was reverting to her wild state, which was natural. "I cannot take this healthy, strong owl and just let her be a pet for your convenience, it's not right and I won't do it" I defiantly stated. Jane glared at me. "Well then, I will take her with me and we shall see about that." She reached for the door and I stopped her. "This is my property and she is in my care, take care not to trespass nor disrupt this rescue," I warned. "I don't want to call the authorities on you". She stomped off in a huff and I nearly crumbled to the ground. My entire body was shaking and although the woman was gone, I feared that she would return and try and steal the owl.

For days I didn't leave the house. Tyto, who was getting wilder with each passing day and hunting, was a tremendous success. "Just a few more days and she can be released" I whispered, "just a few more days".

The Network called about six days after Jane had threatened to take Tyto. They needed me to come and pick up an injured vulture, so I locked the aviary and drove the five blocks to the office. The vulture was young and I knew that I would have to try and tube him, which would be difficult. As I loaded him into my car I saw *her* van pass me. "Oh no you don't". I said aloud. Driving fast I caught up with her just as she was getting out of her van at my house. "I've come for the bird, out of my way Kari, it's mine and I intend to take her" she snarled. "I don't want to call the authorities on you, but you had best leave my property now" I stammered. With wire cutters in one hand and a dog carrier in the other, she pushed past me and went into my back yard, making her way to the aviary. I ran inside and grabbed the phone. My buddy, Officer Ramirez from Animal Control said he would be there in about five minutes and not to get into any tiff with her. As I hung up the phone she cut the lock off the aviary and opened the door, I ran outside just at Tyto swooped past her and into the sky! "This is all your fault, that bird was mine and you ruined her!" she bellowed. I stood looking at her and said, "She was not yours or mine to keep, she belongs to the skies and that is exactly where she has gone". Stepping toward me, I thought she might strike but Officer Ramirez came in the gate and she backed away. "Everything all right here ladies?" he asked. She just pushed past him and huffed out to her van and drove off.

Officer Ramirez didn't say anything about the exchange, but I knew that eventually Jane would be questioned *if* Fish and Game had hard evidence, but that would mean a captive raptor. I shuddered at the thought. Thanking him for coming, I walked him out to his car. "You know, I rescue birds and animals to give them another chance at life and I don't feel good about people keeping perfectly healthy wild birds in captivity. Education birds, I understand because the public and especially youth need to be made aware of our impact on them and their environment. Is there an answer?" I asked. He smiled and looked at me as I took the vulture out of my car.

"Kari, the answer is to rescue, rehab and release, which is what you do very well. Just look at that ugly fellow in your carrier. He's the answer."

Ramirez drove off and I carried the vulture into the backyard. He was stinking to high heaven and I began to laugh. As I placed him in the larger carrier, I looked at him. "So you're the answer, eh?" With that, he regurgitated all over me. Another day, another rescue and this one is a doozie!

Turkey vulture released into the wild

Tyto just a few weeks old, checking me out

Barn owls are given their name because they prefer to nest and live in barns. Their body length is 14-20 inches with a wingspan of 3 ½ feet and they weigh between 8 and 21 ounces, depending on where they live and what they hunt.

Barn owls catch their prey in total darkness using their excellent hearing and can memorize complex sounds associated with a certain type of prey.

We'jom'pi

The boys were laughing as they swung a baseball bat round and round, hitting and knocking a bird from a tree. Their tattoos and clothing suggested that this might be some sort of "jumping in" ritual, but I wouldn't stand for it. I pulled my car over and got out. Fury raged in my face and heart as I watched these young boys beat a helpless bird. Without thinking I ran up and grabbed the bat from the "leader" of the pack and stood staring them down. "What do you think you are doing?" I screamed. "Are you so low that you have to beat a helpless creature to prove your manhood? How dare you!" The leader stood up to me and at that moment I was scared, really scared. He had a knife in his belt and I knew he could use it. But I couldn't back down, I had confronted them and I had to stand up, even if it meant I might get hurt.

"Wha's your beef, lady?" he sneered. "Why do you care what we do?" I looked at him and as calmly as I could I said, "I care about the bird. I rescue abused animals and try and educate people about abuse, it's obvious you could use some of that education." He laughed at me as I stood my ground. My heart was beating so hard that I felt dizzy but I couldn't let them see that I was scared. So I took a deep breath and went over to where the bird lay. I gently picked it up. They boys had broken its wing and it was going into shock. I walked past the ruffians and took the bird to my car, where I placed it in a box with fleece. I closed my door and turned to look at the boys. "I don't know who you are, or why you felt the need to injure an innocent bird, but what you did is wrong. Are you so bored that you need to use violence to make you look like something?" I demanded, nearly out of breath. "Hey, lady, it's just a stupid bird," he said. I fumed as those words were spoken. "How would you like it if something came at you and beat you to the ground? You would fight back, right?" He looked at me and said "Duh, yeah". They all laughed. "This little bird couldn't fight back. You used your anger to hurt something innocent. What in God's name would make anyone do something like this?" I spat out.

One of the younger kids looked at me and came up closer. I stood looking at him. "Why do you rescue animals, why don't you just let them die?" he asked. I knew at that moment I needed to be smart and say something that would make sense to them. Regaining my composure I said, "I rescue them because *every life* is worth saving, even an animals. We are all here on this planet together, it's our job to help each other, not hurt each other." He looked at me and turned to walk back to the group. The leader stood looking at me and quietly asked, "Do you rescue people too?" I took a deep breath and said, "Yes". At that moment it seemed that we all understood each other and my fear melted.

"Look, I need to get this bird home and see if I can save it" I said. I reached in my pocket and took out my card and gave it to the leader. "Maybe you might want to come and see what rescuing is all about, if you have so much time on your hands why not use it to help." He stared at me and I turned to get in my car. The boys stood quietly looking at me and I could see that they realized that they were wrong. I didn't think I would ever hear from them, but I felt the need to at least make the effort to invite them to do something positive.

A few weeks later when I went to the network there was a message for me from Jesus. I didn't know anyone named Jesus but I called him back. It was the leader of the bad boys. "Hey, we been thinking, what we did was wrong, but we don't got any way to do things better." He said. I didn't know what to think or say, but I invited him and his "friends" to come to a presentation I was doing with an owl named We'jom'pi., This owl had been the subject of abuse also and the program was dedicated to education and enlightenment, and it was on Earth Day. He said they would think about it.

The day came for the presentation and I loaded my little owl into the travel carrier. Before I left, I went to the aviary and checked on the bird that had been beaten by the boys. It was a kestrel and surprisingly had healed well. The wing responded to the wrap and within a short amount of time had healed completely so that the bird could fly. I was thrilled that this little thing would have a second chance, despite the circumstances that brought it to me.

We'jom'pi, a western screech owl, was a great traveler. He didn't mind crowds and also didn't mind being taken out during the day. He had also been beaten by someone and had ended up at the network. His wing though could not be repaired and he had many other issues as well. He quickly bonded with the volunteers and preferred our company to that of his own species. So we made him an education bird and took him to schools to teach kids about respecting nature. I was given the honor of keeping him at my home and being his caregiver. I didn't mind because he was very sweet and loving and enjoyed being held. It blew my mind every time I took him out of his mew that I had a screech owl and he let me hold him!

We reached the fairgrounds where the festivities were taking place. Speakers from all over the world had come to celebrate Earth Day and I had been asked to be one of them. It was indeed an honor to be in the company of such revered educators and activists. As I waited my turn I sat with We'jom'pi on my lap. A group of Tibetan monks were up next and they came and sat by me. The innocence of their faces and delight as they touched his tiny feathers was not unlike that of a child at Christmas. They giggled and stood in awe of this tiny little owl.

Their presentation was an ethereal mixture of music and chanting that resonated peace and harmony. I couldn't believe that I was following these men of greatness, my little owl and me. We were introduced and were greeted by a resounding applause. We'jom'pi sat perched on my hand as I talked about his injuries and about walking in peace with nature. He looked around and tilted his head as if acknowledging the people in the vast audience. As I spoke I noticed some familiar faces. The bad boys were in the audience, watching and participating in a day of peace. My heart soared as I continued my brief presentation. I felt that this moment, this day would make an impact on so many lives and that these boys had come to be part of that.

When I had finished I walked off the stage with the sound of applause ringing in my ears. It had been a great presentation and many people cried as I talked about the abuse we humans inflict not only upon our animal friends but to our own kind as well. The boys watched me and I could see they were touched. A Chumash medicine man and dancers who danced in honor of the winged ones followed me. It was a magical day and from backstage I saw the boys smiling and laughing. It was as if this day had healed past wounds and opened up new possibilities. As I sat and enjoyed the rest of the day I was reminded that everyone and everything is worth saving, no matter the circumstances.

The little kestrel that had been beaten, healed and ready to be free

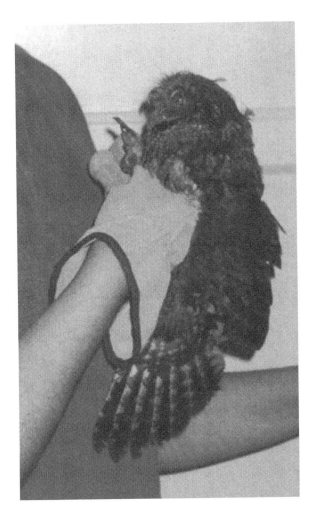

We'jom'pi; a great ambassador of peace

Appendix

My actions are my only true belonging. I cannot escape the consequences of my actions. My actions are a ground upon which I stand.

Thich Nhat Hanh

Rescue Basics

A word of caution: Never approach an injured animal without help, when in doubt walk away or call for back up assistance.

A well-prepared rescuer can often be the difference between life and death in an injured animal. The following are suggestions for you to have on hand. I have my rescue kits in several places so that I always can grab and go if need be. Remember, after the rescue, when you have come home, take stock of your rescue kit and replace any used items and wash all towels and bandages immediately. Disinfect your instruments with a germicide or alcohol and hot water. Following is what I have in my kit after years of trial and error.

Grab and Go Rescue Box

- A sturdy cardboard box with lid, for emergency transport, or containment for transport
- Stethoscope
- Leather gloves
- Goggles
- Slip leash, several
- Plastic disposable eyedroppers
- Small, blunt nosed scissors
- Plastic tweezers, several lengths
- Clean towels four or five
- Soft fleece in solid colors 2'x2'
- Examining gloves (box)
- Hand warmers
- Foot warmers
- Sterile gauze pads, cotton balls, cotton swabs
- Small to medium baby bottles with extra nipples
- White waterproof adhesive tape
- Kotex (without adhesive strip)
- Vet wrap

- Hydrogen peroxide; (squeeze container for easy dispersal)
- Isopropyl alcohol
- Distilled/purified water
- Electrolyte solution
- Betadine solution
- Calendula tincture or ointment
- Triple antibiotic ointment
- Medicated powder
- Bag balm
- Styptic powder
- Temperature strips
- Paper towels
- Large plastic garbage/lawn bags

This may seem like a lot of items, however when on the site of a rescue there is no time to go and get something. Many of these items can be found at dollar stores, just be sure to check for the expiration date.

So, you want to volunteer?

If you like to volunteer and love animals of all kinds; if you are not afraid of being bitten; if you don't need a paycheck and can deal with being dirty and smelly almost every day; then rescue *may* be for you.

Animal rescue is not for the meek. It takes a certain kind of person to be able to handle the crisis situations that come with rescue. What type of person is that? Actually, no one has really figured it out. We are from all walks of life and for the most part, stick with rescue because we love what we do and feel we are making a difference, not matter how small or insignificant.

Training is more hands-on than not and often a person is thrown into a rescue situation with little to no experience. Many believe that is preferable, at least in the beginning. There are no bad habits to be unlearned. If you are thinking of volunteering as a rescuer, here are a few hints to help you on your way. Check your local phone book for Animal Shelters in your area. Give them a call and inquire about their volunteer requirements.

Most shelters are run by volunteers with no paid staff and are most eager to open their doors to anyone willing to volunteer even a couple of hours a week to help the animals. The following are a few things a volunteer can do to help:

1. **Dogs need exercise**. A nice brisk walk a couple of times a week does wonders for the psyche of a dog, not to mention the walker. Many animals suffer from kennel rage. They get depressed and begin acting out. This is not good for the handlers and not good for a prospective adopter. Being walked improves the animal's disposition and gives the volunteer an added boost and fun exercise with the

satisfaction of knowing that you are making a difference in the life of the animal you are walking. Your time could be the key to helping that animal get adopted. Your generosity could be the turning point in a dog's life, so much so that it is rescued from euthanasia.

2. **Petting kitties is good for the soul**. Most cats are somewhat anti-social; however they do crave human contact and being brushed or held is one of the greatest gifts you can give them.

3. **Poop detail.** It's not fun, but it is an important and necessary part of any shelter or rescue. Animals poop and someone has to clean it up. Once you've done it a couple of times, it's really not that bad.

4. **Office stuff.** If you are not into the hands on animal part of rescue, but still want to help, why not volunteer your services in another way? Envelopes need to be stuffed and stamped, signs need to be made, phones are always ringing and offices need to be cleaned. There is *something for anyone* who wants to help, you just need to know what you are good at and volunteer those services.

Wild Things

Locate a rescuer who takes in squirrels, raccoons, exotic birds or whatever. Volunteer your time in cleaning cages, mixing formula, washing bedding or whatever the rescuer needs. The education attained by helping in this capacity is invaluable and will most likely propel you to other rescue endeavors. Be prepared, it's highly addicting!

Most wildlife rescuers are self trained. Some have attended IWRC classes for certification. Usually, you will not be allowed to handle wild animals without supervision at first, but with time and the confidence of the rescuer, perhaps you will be side by side helping in no time.

While it is not mandatory, most rehabbers and rescuers get vaccinated for rabies, hepatitis and update their tetanus vaccination. Precautionary measures always pay off. These vaccinations are expensive, but worth the money in the long run.

Anything you can or want to do will be appreciated by any rescuer. The dedication of these people is mind-boggling and their days are spent from sun up to sundown and beyond caring for abandoned, abused and rescued animals of all kinds. Your time could mean the survival of an animal, and most assuredly it will mean a great deal to an overworked rescuer!

Rat Poison:
Often-fatal results to animals

The information contained in this story is for education purposes only and does not in any way discredit the makers of rodenticides.

Some form of rodent infestation plagues most of us. Whether it is in the barn, garage or even in our homes. Rats and mice spread disease, so we do what we can to rid ourselves of these worrisome pests. However the over-the-counter chemicals that are available contain deadly poisons that can be fatal if consumed by animals.

A very loving and responsible family owns a rescued three-year-old terrier mix named Maggie. She is given the best foods, is annually vaccinated and leads the epitome of a dogs' life with her human companions. Unfortunately, Maggie got into some D-Con. $1,500 later, the dogs life was saved, fortunately, but not without consequences. The effects of rat poison are lingering and most animals, sadly, are diagnosed too late to be treated.

Pend Oreille veterinarians instantly recognized the symptoms and started Maggie on vitamin K. This vitamin, a cousin to vitamin E and A circulates through the blood stream and is activated when needed to form a clot. The rat poison had affected Maggie to the point that she was bleeding internally and her x-Ray showed blood in the lungs and stomach. Maggie was transferred to North Idaho Animal Clinic for a plasma infusion to further coagulate her blood, was given IV fluids and was kept for two nights for observation. Her clotting factors or PTT results were checked during the duration of her stay.

Maggie was released to go home with antibiotics and vitamin K to be taken for the next 3 weeks. The risk for pneumonias was a possible side effect due to the blood in her lungs. Her blood also needed to be continually aided by the vitamin K to ensure she reached the optimum clotting levels. The D-con had reduced her clotting factors to almost non-existent.

- What rat poison does: technically known as anticoagulant rodenticides, the chemicals in rat poison removes the clotting factors in blood and the animals bleed to death internally.

- Symptoms: Most animals do not show signs of poisoning for several days after the toxic dose have been ingested. The slightly obvious signs are weakness and pallor. The gums and tongue are a pale pink color. Bleeding is usually not seen until too late.

- Treatment: if an animal is seen eating the poison, immediate care is needed and a trip to the vet is called for. The vet will most likely induce vomiting and the animal may be given absorbents to help prevent the poison from entering the system. Vitamin K usually will be given for a duration of four weeks to ensure that the animals clotting capability remains stable and no internal bleeding occurs.

- Ecological impact: the diet of raptors (birds of prey) consists mainly of rodents. In raptor rehab, many owls, eagles, hawks and falcons are seen exhibiting the effects of rat poison. While the rehabber does what they can, in most cases the birds suffer and die as a result of consuming a poisoned rodent.

What you can do: use traps instead of poison. Use ultrasonic devices to discourage pests. Have a professional pest remover come in and use proven safe and effective rodent baits that cannot be accidentally ingested by pets.

If you have pets and are using rodent bait, it is imperative that the following be observed to reduce the risk of ingestion and possible death. Pets include: dogs, cats, ferrets, birds, hamsters, gerbils etc.

1. Keep all poisons where pets cannot get to them (Remember, birds, cats, hamsters, ferrets and the like, climb and get into all sorts of places).

2. Monitor the poison baits for dead mice or rats and dispose of immediately.

3. Encourage your pet to not eat without your ok.

Rodenticides without an antidote: The following are not as easily reversed and will most likely lead to a painful death.
Vitamin D Analongs (Rat-b-Gone, Quintox)
Bromethalin
Strychnine (gopher bait)
Zinc Phosphide (gopher bait)

As pet owners, we are responsible for the safety of our animals. Being educated and conscientious is the first step to help reduce and/or eliminate the accidental poisoning of these animals that rely on us for their livelihood. We must take a proactive role in the use of rodenticides and understand the possible life threatening impact they have not only on our own pets, but also to the environment, raptors and other wild animals that consume rodents.

Maggie. What a lucky girl!

Lightning, Firecrackers and other noise phobias

It is unfortunate that many people in their zeal for fun overlook the trauma of fireworks and the affect it has on dogs, cats and horses.

My sister has a golden retriever named Kiowa, the epitome of a loving pet. He really has no bad habits, doesn't chew up anything and is content to have her throw a ball or toy for him. Until fireworks start or there is a thunderstorm. This tenderhearted dog is so traumatized that he hurts himself, running in a panic to escape the noise. In order to protect him, he must be locked up until the noise subsides.

Kiowa is like many animals that are sensitive to the popping of firecrackers or the crashing of thunder. There are ways to help the stress brought on by these noises- homeopathy, aconite and rescue remedy. These offer a curative healing instead of medicating the animal with a synthetic drug that masks the symptom. I have also used with a great deal of success, Calms Forte, a homeopathic treatment that helps take the edge off during a thunder storm or on a holiday such as the Fourth of July. Homeopathy is easy to use, has no side effects and offers at least some relief to lessen the severity of the trauma.

- Aconite addresses fear and prevents shock and can be life supporting on the way to the vet.

- Calms Forte provides a natural sense of calm without drugs and is safe to use over a period of weeks if your animal is suffering from noise related stress.

- Rescue Remedy is a miracle in a bottle. A few drops in the mouth of your pet can greatly reduce anxiety, fear and trauma. It is readily available at health food stores and is safe to use on all pets, even birds and fish.

When we moved from California to Montana I gave my animals, dogs, cats and birds rescue remedy in their water. They all traveled with ease, and did not show signs of trauma during the long drive. This natural remedy does not make them sleepy like a tranquilizer; instead it addresses the fear or stress and makes them calm. A calm pet makes for a calm human!

The use of homeopathy is also encouraged if you have a pet that suffers stress from being left alone. A few drops of rescue remedy given directly will help reduce the stress in your animal and lessen the severity of trauma associated with being left alone. This is particularly effective for Doxies, Chihuahua's, Rat Terriers, Yorkies and Shizus. Another fool-proof way to keep them safe is to keep them inside during thunder storms, the 4th of July or other times when there is a lot of unusual noise that may trigger their phobia.

For more information on ordering Homeopathic treatments please see the resource page of this book.

Kiowa, my sister's dog that suffers from noise phobia.

Rescue Recipes

Homemade Electrolyte Solution
Electrolyte solution replenishes body fluids and is essential to dehydrated and or injured animals. Never administer fluids to an unconscious animal. **<u>Do Not</u>** administer fluids to a bird by mouth (beak) as they are prone to aspiration of fluids. Instead, use one drop of the remedy diluted in water and place in the eye with an eyedropper.

1 part purified water
1 Tbs. raw sugar or honey
1 Tsp table salt

Mix well and place in sterilized plastic bottle. Refrigerate any unused portion. This will keep for up to a week in the refrigerator.

Kitten and Puppy Milk Replacement Formula
Can be used for squirrels and bats also, diluted.

8 oz. organic evaporated milk or goats milk
(Do not use soy milk)
8 oz. fresh purified water
1 egg yolk (discard egg white)
1 Tbs. corn syrup (prevents diarrhea)

Blend together and place in sterilized glass container with lid. Refrigerate and warm only amount to be used. Test on arm to make sure it is not too hot. Do not microwave, this removes positive bacteria needed for digestion.

Bird Rescue Formula I

1 cup good quality dry kitten kibble, (no red dyes) soaked in warm water until soft
1 egg yolk (discard egg white)
1/16th tsp Vita Hawk or other avian vitamin
1/16th tsp corn syrup (to prevent diarrhea)

When kibble is soft, drain any remaining water off and transfer to a blender, add egg yolk and vitamin powder, blend until soft and mushy, but not runny. It should be the consistency of heavy cream. Add more water if too dry.

Store formula in plastic containers in small batches in your freezer for up to six months. Thaw and use as needed.

Bird Rescue Formula II

This is a high protein formula for wild birds. Do not feed to canaries or finches.

Purina high protein kitten kibble soaked in water until soft
3 tsp smooth peanut butter
3 tsp Gerber baby oatmeal cereal
1 banana
3 tsp baby applesauce
3 tsp baby creamed corn
3 tsp baby mixed vegetables
2 tsp plain organic yogurt

When kibble is soft, add remaining ingredients in blender. Pulse until smooth and fluid. Store in plastic container in small batches in the freezer for up to six months. Thaw and use as needed.

Resources

International Wildlife Rehabilitation Council (IWRC)
PO Box 3197
Eugene, OR 97403
(866) 871-1869
www.IWRC.com
The IWRC is a Non-profit professional training organization that is comprised of veterinarians, rehabilitators, conservationists and other professionals from around the world, all committed to restoring health, ensuring the welfare and safeguarding the future of wildlife. They are now offering online courses.

Only Natural Pet Store
(888) 937-6677
www.Onlynaturalpet.com
Extensive holistic healthcare library available online, listing homeopathic formulas for dogs and cats.

Pet Alive
(877) 289-1235
www.naturalremedies.com/petalive
Natural remedies designed for cats and dogs

Bach Flower Remedies for Animals
(866) 467-6444
www.herbalremedies.com/bachflowremfo
Full listing of symptoms with remedies for pets including: horses and other wildlife

All websites and phone numbers were current at time of publication.

Acknowledgements

We are never alone in this world and that is very true for a rescuer. It takes many people to successfully network together to assist animals in need and the true success of a shelter or rehab center is not in the "state of the art equipment" they have (most work out of cold garages, or worse), it is in the camaraderie as a group with a specific goal in mind; help the animals. My thanks go out to the following people, who have gone above and beyond in their call to help the injured animals that cross their paths. May your devoted hearts be forever guided by love and compassion and may you always know, you do make a difference, and it's never a lost cause.

My rescue "sister" **Lenora Jones,** who gives magical healing to stray cats in Ohio. She, on her own currently cares for over 40 rescued cats of all ages and takes each in to be spayed, neutered and leukemia checked. Lenora is a true advocate for abandoned and abused cats and has dedicated her life to saving the unwanted and giving them a quality of life they most likely would never have known.

Irene Matijick: With the laughter of a child and the spirit of a lion, Irene is a true "animal whisperer." She advocates for the right and humane treatment of all animals across the US and opens her home and heart to abused, stray and unwanted critters. Irene trains horses in a loving and gentle manner. She strongly advocates the rights of humans to own wolf or wolf hybrids and is a living testament to their well-being and rich full life.

Cindy Knutsen: 24/7 should be her middle name. Cindy runs a feral catch/spay-neuter and release program both in Washington and North Idaho where she works with people who are without adequate funds to spay and or neuter their pets. Cindy humanely live traps the cats and dogs, drives countless miles and sees that each is cared for. She helps people who have lost their jobs with pet food and gives time and her expertise to shelters when they need assistance with sick or injured cats. She is the epitome of a rescuer and often the only person that stands between someone shooting a feral cat and their salvation.

Pend Oreille Veterinary Clinic: Their fast thinking and use of Vitamin K saved Maggie's life. They are always available to offer assistance either in person or over the phone.

North Idaho Animal Hospital: A state of the art facility in Sandpoint Idaho. This hospital operates 24/7 with a highly trained staff and excellent assistants. They treat domestic and exotic animals.

Erica Ann Fuller: My "niece" is given responsibilities beyond her years. At 15 going on 16, Erica cares for dogs, gives them meds, feeds and waters them and gives them quality time while their owners are away. Erica also is learning to work with children with abuse issues. She has a deep love of animals and children with a natural ability to understand them. She aspires to study to be a veterinarian or pediatrician when she graduates from high school and is an inspiration to young people to be a part of nature.

Thank you **Cynthia and Dennis Merritt** for bringing Reiki to the abused dogs and cats at the shelter. I despaired finding the answer to help them and you brought an approach that truly is energy from above.

Michael Guthrie: Thank you for being such a true friend over the years and for the advice, care and concern you always show. You are the quintessential definition of a friend and will *always* be a part of our life.

Dave and Mary Blanton: The shelter brought us together in the manner of one silly boy named Pepper. Thank you for opening your home to the dogs at the shelter and for giving them such a loving home. We cherish your friendship and love sharing time with you and your critters.

Glenn and Michelle Rohrer: We are blessed to have you in our lives. It was a match made in heaven when you gave Rike a forever home and I enjoy being "Auntie Kari" to your animal babies. Thank you for being such dear friends.

Cathy Reynolds: Your devotion to animals is unselfish. Your dedication to assisting the local shelter goes above and beyond. Thank you for giving of your time to help the animals and for the positive attitude you have, even when the going gets tough. You are appreciated and loved for who you are and what you do.

TLC Bird Haven: A 501 © 3 parrot rescue dedicated to the frequently misunderstood birds that are often subjected to severe abuse. This sanctuary brings healing and love to many beautiful exotics. TLC is looking to build a 60 by 60 facility and needs assistance. Please visit their website at: www.tlcbirdhaven.org

Rosemary Lewis: Thank you for your love and care and for sharing Josie with me. You are a true friend and *the* example of a true southern lady!

Jack Donais: The owner of Bordertown Feed in Priest River Idaho, Jack is a rescuer, helper and friend to animals in need. He is one of the most loving and caring individuals always willing to lend a hand to anyone. Thank you for what you do for our furry and winged friends!

Index

A

abuse, 36-41
alternative healing, 42
animal control, 70
antibiotic, amoxicillin ointment, 137

B

bach flower remedy, 25, 29-30, 33
barn owls, 113
bats, 44-48
betadine solution, 62
bird rescue, formula, 137
bottle feeding: kitten 104, fawn 53, goats 20 squirrel 43

C

cats, 101-106
chihuahua, 107-109
colostrum, 102
crow, 115-118

D

d-con, 137
deer, 52-57
domestic animals, 99, 101, 107

E

ecological impact, 82
electrolytes, 144
environment, changes, pollution 24, 50, 82

F

fish and game, 44
flight aviary, 83, 112, 117

foaling, 20

G

great horned owl, 90
goats milk, 52, 71
garden snake, 19

H

hawks, 80-86
homeopathy, 24, 27 arnica Montana 27, 30, hypericum, 27, 30

I

iguana, 18
imprinting, 108, 113
international wildlife rehabilitation council (IWRC) 26
insectivore, 96

K

kitten milk replacement, 46, 49

M

Mealworms, 28
mice, 19
mutilating, self, 33

N Neurological, 28-30

O

opossum, 31-35, 63-75
owl, 83, 90-94, 112, 117

P

paralysis, 31

R

raccoons, 51-56
reiki, 25, 36-40
recipes , 144-145
rescue remedy, 41
rodenticides, 138

S

swallows, 77-79

T

tube feeding, 84

V

vaccinations, hepatitis, rabies, tetanus, 128
vita hawk, 84
vitamin k, 138

W

wolf advocate, 147
woodpecker, 26-30

Not even a sparrow, worth only half a penny, can fall to the ground without our Father knowing it.

Matthew 10:29

Coming Soon
by

Kari D Thompson

Spice em, dice em and slice em,
Fast, fun and delicious meals in a jiffy.

Micah, the biblical mouse

The adventures of Kayla
and Nibbles,
the Siamese cat

About Angels: An inside look at angel visitations

Theme parties made easy

Made in the USA
San Bernardino, CA
11 July 2017